OPEN AND DISTANCE LEARNING SERIES

Programme Evaluation and Quality

A Comprehensive Guide to Setting up an Evaluation System

JUDITH CALDER

KOGAN PAGE
Published in association with the
Institute of Educational Technology, Open University

Open and Distance Learning Series

Series Editor: Fred Lockwood

Activities in Self-Instructional Text Fred Lockwood
Exploring Open and Distance Learning Derek Rowntree
Improving Your Students' Learning Alistair Morgan
Key Terms and Issues in Open and Distance Learning Barbara Hodgson
Preparing Materials for Open, Distance and Flexible Learning Derek Rowntree
Programme Evaluation and Quality Judith Calder
Teaching Through Projects Jane Henry
Teaching with Audio in Open and Distance Learning Derek Rowntree
Understanding Learners in Open and Distance Education Terry Evans
Using Communications Media in Open and Flexible Learning Derek Rowntree

To my colleagues past and present, from whose pleasure in new ideas I have learned and continue to learn so much.

First published in 1994
Reprinted in 1995 and 1997

Kogan Page Limited
120 Pentonville Road
London N1 9JN

British Library Cataloguing in Publication Data

A CIP record for this book is available from the British Library.

ISBN 0 7494 0847 2

Typeset by BookEns Ltd, Baldock, Herts.
Printed and bound in Great Britain by Biddles Ltd, Guildford and King's Lynn

Contents

Series editor's foreword

The use of open and distance learning is increasing dramatically in all sections of education and training, both in the UK and around the world. Many schools, colleges, universities, companies and organizations are already using open and distance learning practices in their teaching and training and want to develop these further. Furthermore, many individuals have heard about open and distance learning and would welcome the opportunity to find out more about it and explore its potential.

Whatever your current interest in open and distance learning and experience within it, I believe there will be something in this series of short books for you. This series is directed at teachers, trainers, educational advisers, in-house training managers and training consultants involved in designing open and distance learning systems and materials. It will be invaluable for those working in learning environments ranging from industry and commerce to public sector organizations, from schools and colleges to universities.

This series is designed to provide a comprehensive coverage of the field of open and distance learning. Each title focuses on a different aspect of designing and developing open and distance learning and provides concrete advice and information, which is built upon current theory and research in the field and how it relates to actual practice. This basis, of theory, research and development experience, is unique in the area of open and distance learning. I say this with some confidence since the Open University Institute of Educational Technology, from which virtually all the authors are drawn, contains the largest collection of educational technologists (course designers, developers and researchers) in the world. Since the inception of the Open University in 1969 members of the Institute have made a major contribution to the design and production of learning systems and materials not just in the Open University but in many other organizations in this country and elsewhere in the world. We would now like to share our experiences and findings with you.

In this book, *Programme Evaluation and Quality*, Judith Calder presents advice and information which will help you to identify ways in which programme evaluation can be developed to improve internal decision-making and the quality of your provision and to meet a range of both internal and external information needs. Judith systematically explores the context in which those involved in programme evaluation operate. She discusses the main ideas, approaches and practices in the field and acknowledges the pressures under which you and your colleagues operate. The book provides a sound framework within which you can either review your existing programme evaluation provision or assemble one. It also provides numerous examples and illustrations to support the points she makes and to present the advice and information in a concrete and meaningful way.

The book is not just for those in management and administrative positions who are often responsible for instigating, monitoring and reporting on programme evaluations. It will also be of immense value to those teachers and trainers who are involved in some aspect of programme evaluation – or who are thinking of getting involved.

Fred Lockwood

Preface

The growth in open and distance learning during the late eighties and the early nineties reflects the worldwide changes in the way in which post-compulsory education and training is seen. The attempts of educators and trainers to use advances in information and communication technology and in educational thinking to provide education and training which is of benefit to both students and their communities are having to take place against a background of economic cutbacks and increasing competition for resources. Government encouragement to expand and to innovate is accompanied by explicit pressure to prove the worth of what is being achieved.

The aim of this book is to help providers of open and distance learning identify the ways in which programme evaluation can most appropriately help them in meeting both internal and external needs for information, feedback, and insight into the nature and quality of their teaching/training provision. The term programme evaluation is intended to encompass the evaluation for developmental or appraisal purposes of programmes of teaching and training-associated activities and of the courses and teaching-related systems within them. The book is intended for professionals involved in the management, provision or administration of open and distance learning organizations, both in educational establishments and in the workplace. It is intended to help them to assess their own current programme evaluation provision and to review how best to develop the programme evaluation activities in their own organization.

The book covers three broad sets of issues over nine chapters. It opens by looking at the context within which open and distance learning providers are currently operating. It reviews the thinking behind evaluation ideas, and their application to the field of education and training. It also examines the main external pressures which affect evaluation priorities and processes, and considers the range and diversity of the internal programme evaluation needs of open and distance learning providers. Finally comes a review and discussion of the issues which must be considered and the decisions which have to be made in putting together a system of programme evaluation.

The term evaluation means different things to different people. It can be limited by the uses to which it is intended to be put, by the materials, activities or processes on which it focuses, or by the research designs and methodologies that it uses. Chapter 1 lays out the groundwork of the main approaches to evaluation and relates them to different types of information needs within organizations. The concept of formal evaluation as a process is introduced. Its importance in enabling organizations to find out just what being a student within that organization means and the need to use evaluation findings to become a 'learning organization' are discussed.

The wider environment within which open and distance learning institutions have to operate is the focus of the second chapter. Here, the links which new forms of education and training have with the economic agenda of the countries and the communities within which they operate are introduced. The effects of economic pressures on accountability and quality concerns are discussed in the context of their implications for providers' information needs. The extent to which these needs can be met by such means as performance indicators and quality measurement systems and their limitations in helping providers maintain and improve the quality of their provision is discussed. The chapter concludes by looking at the concept of self-evaluation in the form of the organizational learning models outlined by Argyris and Schön (1978).

The theme of the third chapter is that statistics about students and about the clients of open and distance learning organizations should be seen as the foundation of any system of programme evaluation. The argument is put that organizations frequently hold a great deal more data than they are at first aware. The possible sources of existing data and their use as basic evaluation measures are reviewed. One of the major problems in open and distance teaching is in keeping track of the students. Various options are discussed, together with ideas about the sort of data which would provide a useful regular baseline of student progress and outcome statistics.

However useful student statistics are in monitoring what is happening within an organization, they do have limitations. Chapter 4 introduces some ideas about the contribution of different methods to identifying learning and training needs for programme and curriculum development purposes. Examples of major studies are used to illustrate the approaches which can be used in gathering the sort of information needed when making decisions about whether to extend provision to new target groups or to extend the type of provision being offered. The question of how best to establish the viability of the new or revised programmes is discussed. Both pump-priming and piloting are approaches which have been used extensively, and the chapter concludes by examining successful examples of each.

Central to the success of any programme of studies are courses which meet the needs of the students and of any sponsors there may be. Chapter 5 examines the contribution which programme evaluation can make at the course design, development and presentation stages in order to improve their quality and teaching effectiveness. The frequent separation of course design and development from the teaching and learning stage found in much open and distance teaching accentuates the need for systematic forms of feedback. A wide selection of methodological approaches and tools have been developed for use by course designers and developers. It has to be recognized that none of the major approaches reviewed in this chapter is ideal. Nevertheless, the range of possibilities outlined should enable designers to find an approach which meets at least some of their needs. Similarly, the examples of feedback instruments included in the chapter have been selected in order to illustrate how the question of who carries out the evaluation and its purpose can affect the types of questions asked and the way they are asked.

While the course is usually the focal point of the programme provision, the students' experiences are determined by the sum total of all their interactions with the organization which is providing the course. This starts with their awareness of what it has to offer which is relevant for their needs, and lasts through to aspects such as the way their enquiries about assignments are handled, the accessibility of their tutors and the general 'user friendliness' of the organizational procedures and regulations. Chapter 6 examines the ways in which programme evaluation can be used to gain a better understanding of how the students view the different services, and what problems they may encounter. Three common monitoring approaches are described and reviewed with the strengths and weaknesses of each identified.

In Chapter 7, we move on to the issues involved in setting up a system of programme evaluation. This chapter focuses on the nature of the system which is to be established. The different options which are possible in terms of defining the purposes, priorities and policies of such a system are many, and the final choice has to be made by those who understand the needs of the organization in the form of the potential clients of the evaluation work. There are no clear-cut answers to the question of who should actually carry out the research and evaluation activities. The review of the main options in terms of internal versus external people suggests that the optimal approach is likely to be some form of mix, depending on local circumstances.

Once the purposes of the programme evaluation are agreed, there remains the question of just how they are to be achieved. Chapter 8 reviews and discusses the different types of research and monitoring studies, methodologies and research instruments available for programme evaluation. The need for multiple usage of data in order to minimize the collection costs is a lesson which needs constant reiteration. New problems always bring with them the desire to be seen to be doing something by collecting data. The careful review of existing data has far less obvious appeal, yet the bringing together of data from different sources can often result in stronger, more reliable conclusions. This in turn highlights the need for a certain level of investment by the organization in order to set up and then maintain a minimum programme evaluation capability. Clearly the level of this investment will vary substantially depending on the nature of the programme evaluation system for which an organization opts. However a brief review of the main types of resources to which access is needed and suggestions on a timetable for implementing a full system should help readers in their detailed planning.

The final stage in the setting up of a system of programme evaluation is when it comes to determining whether or not it is achieving its purposes. The ninth and final chapter takes the reader through all the sequences of a self-evaluation for a system of programme evaluation. Picking up on the theme of the learning organization which was introduced in the first chapter, the aim is to set in place from the very beginning the capacity and the procedures for self-monitoring and reflection which will enable the system to be both flexible and responsive to changes in the needs of the organization and in the constraints within which it must operate.

Too often in the past there has been a tendency on the part of senior management to see resources for evaluation as an optional extra which, if necessary, can be put to one side. The changes in the demands of funding bodies for greater public accountability from those in receipt of public funds is changing this attitude. However, the vice-chancellor of the UK Open University highlighted the fact that there is still a problem with matching needs and plans with resources. He drew attention to the phenomenon of *pryoectismo,* described by Rumble as 'the elaboration of ambitious plans out of all proportion to the resources available' (Daniel 1989). The aim then must be to develop plans for programme evaluation which while ambitious and forward looking in their purposes, are designed to develop at a rate which recognizes the realities of resource availability.

Acknowledgements

I would like to express my thanks to all those who helped in bringing this book to fruition. In particular to Fred Lockwood, whose idea it all was, and who provided the energy and enthusiasm to turn the plans into reality; Helen Carley, Commissioning Editor at Kogan Page, for her patience and support; and to my colleagues Alison Ashby for her comments on early drafts, together with Adrian Kirkwood, Beryl Crooks, Angie Ballard, John Brennan and Derek Rowntree for their ideas and advice. I would also like to thank my family for their encouragement and support and for the computing back-up expertise they provided.

Chapter 1

The nature of evaluation

Think about the last time that you considered the need to make some sort of change. Before choosing a particular course of action, you would have reviewed the available options, or at least the options that you knew about. You would have assessed how well each option might meet your needs, and at what cost. You would then have weighed up the advantages and disadvantages associated with each of the options before making your decision.

The change you selected might have been about some personal matter such as your family finances, or something to do with your children's future. Or it may just as easily have been related to your professional life. You may have been thinking about introducing a new course, or modifying the student registration system, or increasing student retention. Whatever your area of concern, in order to carry out any change, you will have had to work through the process which we call evaluation.

The process of evaluation which we employ to reach a decision as to the way forward is the same regardless of the area of concern or its source or even of its importance. The care we take, the methods we use and the amount of attention we give to the process in those different situations is another matter. In this chapter we will be looking at formal evaluation, considering the purpose of formal evaluation activities in open and distance teaching organizations and examining the different types of approaches to evaluation which are available to us.

Formal evaluation

Evaluation then is an activity with which everyone is familiar. The question is, how you can best use evaluation with open and distance learning provision. At the informal level, individual members of any institution will be actively engaged in making their own personal evaluations of activities which come within their own areas of responsibility. The problem will be that, as with all other spheres of life, individuals' perceptions will be coloured and distorted by the particular lenses through which they see the world. We can only make an evaluation on the basis of the information to which we have access. The conclusions that we reach will be limited by the quality of that information — its comprehensiveness, relevance, up-to-dateness, accuracy.

A more structured approach

One way of looking at the process of evaluation is to view it as a series of different stages. The stages which comprise this cycle are shown in Figure 1.1. It should be emphasized that reality is usually much more untidy and idiosyncratic. Some stages may be omitted, and the sequencing may not always operate as shown. The old joke about deciding what the conclusions will be before carrying out the evaluation does, as is often the case, carry a grain of truth. For example political pressures may result in stage 7 actions being agreed on political grounds before the evaluation findings in stage 6 are available (a frequent habit with government departments).

Evaluation stages

1 Identify an area of concern
2 Decide whether to proceed
3 Investigate identified issues
4 Analyse findings
5 Interpret findings
6 Disseminate findings and recommendations
7 Review the response to the findings and recommendations and agree any corrective actions
8 Implement agreed actions

Figure 1.1 *The basic stages of evaluation*

Identify an area of concern

This stage can be triggered in a number of different ways. Formal monitoring procedures such as reviews of pass rates, or course registration figures often identify situations which should be giving cause for concern. Informal means such as letters of complaint, or anxieties expressed by staff can lead to the recognition of the existence of possible problem areas. Cost concerns may result in pressure within the organization for the evaluation of a specific project or innovation, such as the use of interactive video for example. Or again there may be an institutional commitment to provide certain data or certain types of evaluation for external auditing, review or grant awarding purposes. If you think of your own institution, you can probably think of just as many if not more instances where the evaluation process has been triggered by external requests for data or because of political pressure than through the process of objective review. The trigger for the evaluation cycle may therefore operate in a variety of ways.

Decide whether to proceed

Not all problems or potential problems which are identified will be seen as having a sufficiently high priority to warrant further investigation. A decision will therefore need to be taken about whether or not to investigate further, or whether to commit resources for a thorough evaluation.

Investigate identified issues

The ways in which issues are investigated should, wherever possible, be determined by the requirements of the problem. For example, the evaluation of an issue such as the quality of guidance to tutors may be usefully approached using a mixture of in-depth discussion to establish the criteria used by the tutors themselves, plus some quantitative feedback to establish the scale of any particular problem areas.

Analyse findings

Whatever the type of study devised and carried out for the evaluation, the data collected need to go through some form of analysis stage. The extent and depth of the analysis will depend in part on the technical competence and in part on the specific interests and institutional requirements of those carrying it out. I have known examples where the analysis of course feedback data was limited simply to a one-page summary of students' written comments presented as a report from the teaching team to 'higher authorities'. I have also seen examples where weeks of sophisticated computer analysis were carried out on complex quantitative data in order to help the course team pinpoint the precise sources of students' problems with a course.

Interpret findings

The more sophisticated and complex the study, the more important is the interpretation phase. The same set of analyses may well be interpreted in very different ways depending on the particular perspective of the interpreter. A high difficulty rating for a course module may be interpreted as evidence that the teaching approach needs further investigation and possibly some revision, or it may be taken as evidence that the students are insufficiently prepared for the course.

Disseminate findings and recommendations

The dissemination phase can be key in determining whether or not the evaluation findings are used. The timing of the dissemination, the target group for the findings, and the perceived relevance of the findings to people's concerns will all need to be taken into account. For example, the importance of variations in student retention rates may be different for those responsible for ensuring the viability of future courses than for administrators responsible for ensuring adequate provision of exam rooms. The same set of information can carry very different messages to different groups. Increased student retention rates may be good news to some staff in an organization, and a mixed blessing to others.

Review findings, agree and implement corrective actions

These final two stages do need to be seen as part of the evaluation process. Evaluation is not an abstract research exercise but an essential tool of good management. In general the methodologies for the design and implementation of evaluation studies are well developed, but the methodologies for enhancing the likelihood of organizational use of evaluation findings is still developing. Hence the importance of recognizing that these two stages must be included in the cycle.

The purpose of evaluation

The aim of evaluation in the case of any organization must be to support that organization in achieving its goals. In other words, to enable it to become a more effective organization within whatever constraints it has to operate. In educational organizations, the need for formal evaluation activities is usually clearly recognized. In their 1977 review of major evaluation studies, Guttentag and Saar drew attention to the fact that 'education is one of the most highly researched evaluation fields' (Guttentag and Saar 1977).

The learning organization

Evaluation is used, or should be used, to enable institutions to operate as learning organizations. The importance of the role of the detection and correction of error is the basis for the ideas on organizational learning put forward by Argyris and Schön (1978). An important feature of their argument is the view of the organization as a unit or a whole in respect of the reviews of performance and the implementation of subsequent modifications.

For example, individuals or small groups such as course teams may have learnt that the submission rates on assignments for a particular course drop sharply at a certain point. There are a number of possible explanations for this phenomenon which would have to be investigated. It may be to do with the difficulty of the assignment or the course workload at that point. If that is the case, then the person responsible for the course will probably attempt to deal with the problem by changing the assignment or by cutting out some of the student study tasks. However, there may be institutional-level implications for this state of affairs. For example, the number of assignments which students are expected to complete, the monitoring of standards, the course approval strategy and the course testing strategies are all aspects where the institutional procedures may have to be modified if the problem is found to be sufficiently widespread or severe.

Programme evaluation

Programme evaluation in the field of open and distance teaching is relatively underdeveloped. By programme evaluation I mean evaluation which focuses on programmes of study. It is at this level that the pedagogic, management and often the financial responsibilities lie in education and training. It is usually here that responsibility for the detailed issues of quality and accountability have to exercised.

I have chosen the term 'programme of study' to describe sets or groupings of courses. Usually, these would be sets of courses which share some sort of common aim. That aim may be the award of a qualification for students who successfully complete a requisite number or series of courses in an area of expertise; or it may be that a particular audience is targeted, or a particular teaching medium is used.

Within any institution it would be a simple if onerous task to list large numbers of possible issues to which evaluation could make some contribution. However 'busyness' is no substitute for purposeful intervention at key points. The question then is how to determine what the key points are — how are we to identify the purposes of evaluation in such a way as to achieve the best match with the goals of the institution?

Diverse institutional goals

The overarching aims of a provider of education will be related to the provision of learning opportunities and to such associated activities as the accreditation of learning. But such global aims can also contain a diverse range of subsidiary goals. In an earlier work I discussed the different types of goals that learning providers can hold (Calder 1993). Four distinct groupings can be identified:

- society/economy centred
- institution centred
- subject centred
- learner centred.

The society/economy centred goals refers to the skill centred education and training which both public and commercial providers are increasingly encouraged to offer. Institutional goals can include institutional survival; high status among clients, other providers or funders; or public recognition. Providers may also hold 'subject centred' goals, by which I mean claims to scholarship and the desire to provide courses of a high academic quality. The learner centred goals emphasize the personal development aspect of learning and the need for learners to achieve not only subject knowledge and skills but also more sophisticated learning strategies and such intangible outcomes as self confidence, recognition of self worth, and a commitment to the community.

You may have noted the absence of student performance from the list. In the UK, the assessment of student performance is referred to by the term 'assessment'. The term 'evaluation' refers primarily to the evaluation of the teaching and organization activities which support student learning and includes the assessment of student performance as just one aspect or function. However in his book on the assessment of students, Rowntree highlights the fact that assessment and evaluation are often treated as 'virtual synonyms'. As he points out, there are many countries, including the USA, where the term 'evaluation' is used to describe both the assessment of individual student performance in terms of what they have learnt or accomplished and the evaluation of the teaching and other organizational activities which support student learning (Rowntree 1977). In fact some institutions use the term 'evaluation' solely to describe the assessment of student performance.

Needless to say, such differences in the the way the term is used can on occasion lead to considerable confusion. Discussions about 'evaluation' between professionals from countries separated by different traditions of usage of the same term can be enlivened by the misunderstandings caused by failure to check on the definitions of apparently common terminology. In this book, I will stay with the UK meaning of evaluation.

Diverse interest groups

The particular interest group which sponsors the evaluation is of particular importance in determining the purpose of any particular evaluation activity. Kogan (1989) described well the complexity of the way in which the nature of the evaluation is determined when he commented that

> The nature of the evaluation will vary according to whether an intervention is primarily directed to, for example, improvements in quality, reduction in cost, equalisation of access, or improvements in working conditions; and it will also vary according to its sponsors whether they be managers, political leaders, client groups, or the workers who are subject to the evaluation.

What Kogan was drawing attention to was that evaluation is not a clear-cut straightforward activity. Rather the primary purpose of the evaluation and the particular interests of the sponsoring group initiating or sanctioning the evaluation will combine to define what kind of approach, what kind of focus the evaluation will have.

Even where the evaluation is commissioned internally and carried out internally, there may still be great differences in its nature. Consider for example, a situation where the quality of the teaching received by students is being evaluated. If the aim of the evaluation is to assist with staff development, then its nature will be rather different than if its aim was to collect data to use for staff appraisals. This particular example is an important one because many staff have relatively little experience with open and distance teaching, and are frequently unaware of the rather different needs of home-based or 'distance' students from those of conventional students or trainees. Certainly the system of student feedback on teaching used by many providers for assessing face-to-teaching can conflict with the need to use evaluation for staff development purposes.

Approaches to evaluation

We have discussed the fact that evaluation is a process which can be utilized across the whole range of activities in an educational institution. The multiplicity of approaches on which it can draw matches the multiplicity of activities with which it can help. One way of looking at these different approaches is to consider the fundamental purpose of the evaluation.

Summative and formative evaluation

Summative evaluation

Where the intention is to form a judgement or conclusion about either the absolute or the relative merits of whatever is the focus of the evaluation, this would be seen as summative evaluation. Scriven (1967), who first advanced the distinction between formative and summative evaluation related it to the effectiveness of the instruction or teaching. It could equally well be used in relation to judging whether a teaching component or some aspect of the student support system has worked as intended. A public examination is another example of a summative evaluation of the candidates' knowledge. Summative evaluations are generally used in order to compare the success of different approaches in achieving a particular goal, or meeting a particular need. Consider the following comment by Nigel Paine (1990) who reviewed the final report of the Open Tech Programme development review:

I wanted to know the answers to some very basic questions:

- how much did it cost?
- what did it achieve?
- what lessons were learnt for the future?
- is this kind of development programme a model for us?

The approach being taken here was very much a summative one. In fact, as Paine pointed out, the development review had been carried out with a distinctly formative focus. This meant that although much of the information needed for a summative evaluation was available, it was used, interpreted and presented with a development focus.

Formative evaluation

Evaluation is formative when it is used with the intention of developing or improving the functioning of an activity or the effectiveness of a component. Testing of instructional materials during their development in order to identify areas where improvements might be made; trials of systems in order to iron out the wrinkles before adopting them fully; reviews of monitoring data carried out in order to identify areas of weakness and establish priorities for improvement would all be classified as formative evaluation.

Evaluation Purpose	Materials Development Phase	Materials Presentation Phase
Formative	Developmental testing	Rolling remake
Summative	Market testing	Validation review

Figure 1.2 *Examples of activities with different evaluation purposes at different materials production phases*

It would be a mistake, however, to think of the distinction between the two forms of evaluation as formative if carried out during the development phase and summative if carried out during the presentation phase. Figure 1.2 shows examples of both formative and summative approaches being used during materials development and materials presentation stages.

In a similar way, material which is gathered for formative purposes may be used for summative decisions, just as data which is gathered for summative purposes can be and often is used in formative ways. Tessmer, in his book on formative evaluation, points out how 'As long as the purpose of the evaluation is to "revise" the instruction by reorganizing or supplanting it, the evaluation can be a type of formative evaluation' (Tessmer 1993). He gives the example of instructors who may wish to evaluate a 'bought in' course. If they intend to modify or supplement those parts which they consider inadequate for their learners, then they would be carrying out a formative evaluation. There is also the point, however, that if it fell below the expected standard, whether technically, pedagogically or academically, then it might be expected that the instructor would decide not to use it at all. In other words, the evaluation would be transformed into a summative evaluation.

Context, input, process and product

Pretest – posttest approach
The next step to consider is what methods of enquiry you can actually use in carrying out evaluations. There is a long tradition of trying to set up experimental designs, or the nearest thing to them that was actually feasible,

in education and media research. However this approach does have limitations because of the problems of trying to control all the variables except for the experimental one. It is also open to criticism about the appropriateness of the 'lab-based' approach for investigating the effectiveness of instructional materials used by different kinds of people in different ways and in different settings. However, variations of it are still used for the formative development of instructional materials. Barbara Flagg (1990) describes a typical pretest-posttest investigation which was designed to look objectively and in detail at what pupils had learnt as a result of the use of videotapes and print materials:

> An example of the one-group pretest-posttest design is the formative evaluation of Systems Impact's prototype videodisc lessons on fractions. . . Teachers presented a series of daily lessons on fractions using videotapes and print materials to mimic the instructional design of the Level 1 videodisc.

> Criterion-referenced tests[1] integrated into every fifth lesson and comprehensive pre- and posttests established the degree of mastery of the fraction concepts. These tests gave evidence as to what programme content was or was not being successfully communicated.

Figure 1.3 illustrates this approach. As you can see, the learning experience, together with any other events or processes which might take place between the pretest and the posttest are not taken account of. In effect, the interaction of the students with the programme is treated as if it were a black box.

Pretest   Programme   Posttest

Figure 1.3 *The pretest-posttest approach*

This approach does have a number of methodological drawbacks. Flagg describes problems such as the drop-out from the test group, possible effects of external events, such as TV maths programmes at home, or extra help from parents, and the effect on the group of constant testing. As Flagg points out 'The pretest-posttest objectives-based study has limitations, . . . in its utility for formative evaluation because it provides little insight as to *why* the programme might be working or might not be working.'

---

1 Criterion-referenced measures assess a student's achievement of subject matter or a student's behaviours in relation to a criterion standard of performance, not in relation to the performance of other students on the same test.

Illuminative evaluation

Concerns about methodological problems and the recognition of the importance of understanding more about the process which the learner was actually going through led to the development of a very different methodological approach, namely illuminative evaluation. Parlett and Hamilton (1972) who developed and introduced this approach saw the pretest-posttest approach as 'a paradigm for plants, not people'. They wrote:

> such evaluations are inadequate for elucidating the complex problem areas they confront and as a result provide little effective input to the decision-making process.

> Illuminative evaluation is introduced as belonging to a contrasting 'anthropological' research paradigm. Attempted measurement of 'educational products' is abandoned for intensive study of the programme as a whole: its rationale and evolution, its operations, achievements, and difficulties. The innovation is not examined in isolation but in the school context or 'learning milieu'.

They explain:

> Observation, interviews with participants (students, instructors, administrators and others), questionnaires, and analysis of documents and background information are all combined to help 'illuminate' problems, issues, and significant program features.

What Parlett and Hamilton were identifying was the importance of the process as well as the input and the outcome. There is also a recognition of the importance of the context in which the learning occurs. Figure 1.4 illustrates the illuminative approach.

Clearly there are limits within programme evaluation as to how much of the programme as a whole can or should be evaluated over extended periods. The illuminative approach was developed very much as a response to the 'agricultural–botanical' approach which had previously predominated. The concern with description and interpretation rather than measurement and prediction, however, reflected a substantial shift in evaluators' understanding of the potential of formal evaluation as an aid to decision-making through greater understanding of what happened within educational programmes.

The CIPP approach

For the evaluation of some projects, an evaluation of the context in which it is operating is essential. A major evaluation of the use of the Canadian Hermes satellite for educational purposes in the late seventies drew

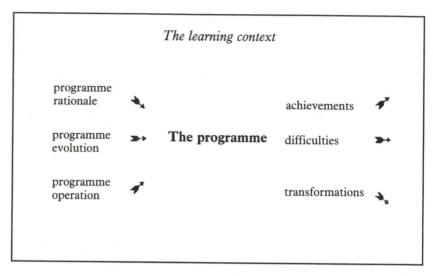

Figure 1.4 *Illuminative evaluation*

particular attention to this aspect. As the evaluators explained:

> The importance of context in educational satellite projects is such that all evaluations must be partly illuminative, even if they rely heavily on survey methods. The study of context involves looking at the costs of the project and the manner in which it was managed. Although such issues are fraught with controversy, knowledge of them is essential to a fair assessment of an experiment. (Richmond and Daniel 1979)

The evaluation framework which was chosen for this massive project was the CIPP approach put together by Stufflebeam and his colleagues (Stufflebeam et al 1971). Richmond and Daniel explain how this acronym describes the four evaluation stages which can encompass the main aspects of the presentation of a course, programme of studies or major project.

Context evaluation: Descriptive data about the programme objectives, intended outcomes, criterion measures.

Input evaluation: The selected programme strategy.

Process evaluation: The implementation of the programme procedures and strategies.

Product evaluation: The success of the programme. (The same as summative evaluation.)

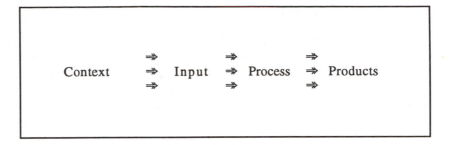

Figure 1.5 *The CIPP evaluation model*

The advantage of the CIPP approach is its comprehensiveness. The example given is of a major national multi-programme project, but the approach is one which can be usefully drawn on even for small studies such as a course or even a module evaluation.

Other approaches
We have looked at the main key evaluation approaches, but in practice there are a whole range of different approaches whose usefulness will depend on the particular concerns you have and on which you want the evaluation to shed light. New approaches to evaluation continue to be developed. With open and distance teaching, the role of evaluation as communication between organization, students and tutors becomes more important. Similarly, developments in research methodology also open up new ways of looking at evaluation. For example, the developments in participative research give respondents more power and a greater say in the research process. In the evaluation context this approach can be seen as a development of the illuminative process. We will be looking at some examples of this approach in Chapter 7.

Utilization of evaluation

The final and often neglected phase of evaluation is its utilization. Within institutional evaluation especially, the view of evaluation as an activity which is completed when the final presentation is made, or the report is presented, is too limiting. The circle must be squared by looking at utilization as part of the evaluation process. This final phase is essential if the institution wishes to identify itself as a 'learning organization'.

The need to take seriously the issue of when and how evaluation findings are used by the organization is highlighted by the experience of those innumerable organizations who have participated in evaluations of various kinds. A report from the Centre for Higher Education Policy Studies (CHEPS) in the Netherlands made the distinction between three types of results arising out of the evaluation activities associated with their quality assessment system: *no utilization, passive utilization* and *active utilization* (Westerheijden, Weusthof and Fredericks 1992).

No utilization
'No utilization' describes the situation where the organization takes no account whatever of the evaluation findings. This situation is, unfortunately, not unusual. Many readers will, I am sure, have shared my experience of having seen decisions taken just before the completion of a major, carefully designed and carried out evaluation study! In such situations, the evaluation report may not even be formally considered within the organization, but merely be put on a shelf, or lodged in a library.

Passive utilization
'Passive utilization' describes the situation where the evaluation findings are formally received and discussed within the institution, without any actions being taken to change anything directly as a result of the evaluation study. The report may be formally disseminated, may be discussed in committee, and may even be the basis for recommendations for a variety of future changes.

Active utilization
Only activity which takes place as a direct result of evaluation findings can be classified as 'active utilization'. Thus if a course evaluation suggests that a particular part of the course is presenting students with difficulties, and as a result, that course is modified, then this would be seen as 'active utilization'.

As Westerheijden et al suggest, this classification refers to the short-term use of evaluation. Very often the relevance and the implications of evaluation findings are not taken up institutionally for some time, but nevertheless, the information and insights from the evaluation may affect thinking within the organization to a considerable degree. You may be able to think of some instances where you have had this experience yourself.

While the worst instances of the lack of utilization of evaluation findings are often found in studies which are carried out by individuals or groups external to the institution this need not always be the case. Utilization can fail to take place regardless of whether the sponsoring group for an evaluation activity is internal or external to the organization; the evaluation activities are carried out by individuals or groups who are internal or external to the organization.

The need for agreed procedures for dealing with the conclusions and recommendations from evaluation studies which are linked with the decision-making structure of the organization is clear. Otherwise, whoever the sponsors are and whoever the evaluators are, it can be too easy for the findings of the evaluation to be set aside.

Conclusion

These developments are part of the growing recognition that no stage of the collection, analysis or utilization of data is a value-free activity. The decision to collect information about, say, the age of students, means that the institution considers this data relevant and important. Equally, the decision not to collect data – about dependent relatives, for example – means that this information is not seen to be of importance to the evaluators (although it may be of considerable importance to students who have to make arrangements to get to study centres or to attend residential schools). Such data may be used either formatively, in that the institution may use them in planning or designing provision which is more appropriate to students needs, or summatively, as in monitoring whether certain agreed admission targets have been met.

We must therefore come to the conclusion that not only does 'evaluation' mean different things to different people, but that its definition depends on one's philosophy of education and on how one intends to use the acquired evaluation information. The information which is available about evaluation approaches reflects very much, as might be expected, the predominant concerns and cultural values of the time. So in education, for example, it could be argued that concerns about the quality of the learning experience for students have, to a considerable extent, been superseded by concerns about the efficiency of the providers.

Much of the early evaluation work in the field of education and training was concerned with judging the outcomes from innovative experimental projects. Kogan (1989) refers to the 'massive American literature concerned with the evaluation of large-scale experiments which are undertaken under controlled conditions in order to note the effects of systematically controlled change.' However, the institutionalization of much evaluation has led to the development of a greater range of evaluation approaches in response both to the identification of a range of evaluation needs at different levels in organizations, and to pressures from inside and outside organizations for more substantial information to assist decision-making at all levels.

In educational research, the implications of the context in which learning takes place for the way we look at the way students learn have long been recognized. With organizations, the model still holds. No provider operates in a vacuum. Just as we need to look at learners' personalities and the wider environment in which they live and work in order to understand their study behaviour, so we need to be aware of the ethos of individual organizations, and the external environment within which they must operate in order to appreciate their organizational behaviour. In the next chapter, we shall be looking at the wider environment in which providers of open and distance learning have to operate and at some of the implications of current trends for programme evaluation.

Chapter 2

The wider environment and evaluation

In this chapter we examine the ways in which changes in the external environment have affected providers of open and distance learning and the consequent effects on providers' evaluation priorities and processes. We will be looking in particular at the implications for programme evaluation of the pressures to identify and collect performance indicators and measures of quality.

The external environment

Links with the economic agenda

At a world conference on distance education in 1992, Lucille Pacey argued that although the linkage between education and training with the economic agenda of countries had always been assumed, this relationship was now being made explicit by governments, businesses and unions. As she put it: 'Our political leaders have targeted education as a lifeline to economic prosperity, recognising the need to emphasise training and education' (Pacey 1992).

The importance of open and distance provision in enabling providers to respond to this linkage with the economic agenda shows itself in a variety of ways. Two of the key types of economic change which most directly affect education and training providers are

- changes in existing industries, with a greater emphasis on competitiveness, productivity and flexibility; and
- structural changes in the labour market with 'old' industries contracting and new industries being developed.

Changes in existing industries to achieve greater competitiveness have involved the shedding of surplus staff, the recruitment of new staff with more appropriate skills and knowledge, and a greater emphasis on the skills, competencies and flexibility of existing staff.

Structural changes in the labour market have the effect of making large numbers of employees in the 'old' industries redundant. These people need a variety of support and help in adjusting to the changes to their personal circumstances and in acquiring skills for finding new jobs for which in turn they may need very different skills. At the same time, the new industries will require a competent trained workforce. If the industry is to develop rapidly, the workforce will either need to be recruited from those who already have the requisite skills or they will need to be trained to the appropriate level of competence in as short a period of time as possible.

Technological developments

At the same time, the number of audio-visual media suitable for distance education has been increasing rapidly. In 1970, the first students with the UK Open University (OU) were offered four courses which between them used print, radio, television, photographic slides, gramophone records, specially designed home experiment kits, face-to-face and telephone tuition and counselling support, and a one-week residential school. By 1993, the media being used had expanded to include home computers, computer links through modems to mainframe computers, computer networking with other computer users, audio cassettes, video-cassettes and videodiscs, and telephone conferencing. There is already some limited use of CD-ROM for services to other institutions and the potential and use of Hypermedia is being investigated (Jones et al 1992).

However, if current usage rather then potential usage is considered, it becomes clear that the particular technologies chosen for teaching reflect student access, cultural preferences and the suitability of national infrastructures for distance education. In many countries in the West and in countries such as India, Sri Lanka, Costa Rica and Pakistan the key medium is still print, although how long this will remain the case is difficult to say. In China, television is the lead medium, with print currently used as a supplement; in Africa the lead medium is often radio, while in the West Indies and in the South Pacific, teleconferencing plays a major role.

Growth of open and distance learning

Perhaps the most visible effect of technological developments on education and training over the last 20 years has been the adoption and growth of distance education. In many countries whole new institutions have been set up as well as open and distance teaching units or schools of distance education being added to existing organizations. New types of provision have been and are being developed in order to meet the new types of demand. For example

- In Australia, open and distance teaching is now being used to provide in-service induction of new workers, to speed up the rate at which they acquire competencies in their jobs (eg a training programme for new graduates in the electricity industry in Queensland, Australia), and training of existing workers to raise the general skills levels (eg training of mill production workers in the Australian Pulp and Paper industry).
- In Venezuela, distance training is being used to train large numbers of workers in diverse locations to support 'significant growth in the country's petro-chemical industry during the 1990's' (Finol 1992).
- Structural changes in the labour market in Sweden have led to increased demands for up-to-date, high quality, intensive retraining courses. The National Institute for Distance Education in Harnossand in Sweden provides an example of one approach devised to meet the needs of both unemployed people and of potentially redundant workers which uses a mixture of short intensive periods of face-to-face tuition, mixed with distance study (Sahlin 1992).

Other changes within the world of education and training in the UK itself include the expansion of provision, both through the growth and development of existing agencies and institutions and through the setting up of whole new ones. Providers now include both public and private organizations who may offer in-service training, in-house company training, open entry and selective entry education and training opportunities. They offer an increasing mixture of initial education, professional education, vocational training, retraining, and updating courses. There have been major new developments in the curriculum and in the type of accreditation offered by institutions. The provision of initial training for graduates to become teachers by the OU was specifically funded by the UK government as a cost-effective way of meeting fluctuating national needs.

At the same time there have been changes in the student bodies, with a much greater percentage of first-generation students receiving education beyond the bare minimum and a greater proportion of mature students. The need of governments for flexible, highly skilled, and well-educated workforces has demanded radical approaches to the variety and types of provision for education and training.

Accountability and quality concerns

Effects of economic pressures

> The increasing reliance on education as an economic tool has not necessarily resulted in any increase in the financial support available to education.

> > The economic crisis . . . has had a particularly damaging effect on higher education in the region. The universities, depending predominantly on government subventions, are faced with a situation in which the grants which governments are able to make available to them are dwindling in real terms from year to year while at the same time there are increasing and competing demands for the services of the institutions. (AAU 1991)

> This extract is from a report on cost effectiveness and efficiency in African Universities. The situation it describes, however, can be found almost anywhere. The competition for resources increases pressure on education and training to show that it is efficient, and that it gives value for money. Increased competition among providers for limited funds leads to further concerns that the quality of provision should be seen not to suffer.

Implications for providers' information needs

> Rapid changes in the wider environment are now a fact of life with which providers of open and distance education must learn to deal. You might like to reflect on the effect of changes in the wider environment on your own institution or unit.

> The pressures on already overstretched public funds has led to an unprecedented demand for public accountability for the use of those resources. Bernadette Robinson has drawn attention to the effects of what she terms

> > an increasingly market-driven approach to education, from demand for public accountability for the use of limited resources and from concern for the maintenance of quality as student populations expand without similarly expanded resource allocation. Particularly in relation to expansion, the effective management of education systems is seen as having a key role in the *maintenance* of quality. (Robinson 1992)

> The effects are already visible and widespread across different types of

providers and different countries. Providers are now frequently expected not only to be accountable to their various funding and management bodies but also to justify their use of the resources that they receive and to demonstrate increasing efficiency and effectiveness while showing evidence that the quality of provision is being maintained.

Effectiveness and efficiency

To demonstrate effectiveness, it must be shown that goals are met. This means that goals need to be made explicit. If one of your goals is to recruit equal numbers of men and women, or certain proportions of different ethnic or religious groups, then the measures you need in order to demonstrate effectiveness with respect to that goal are readily identifiable.

To demonstrate efficiency on the other hand, you have to show that you are making good use of the resources available. It may be that you are an extremely effective provider with respect to recruiting target numbers of students for different courses, but that you achieve this only at some considerable cost. The problem with establishing efficiency is that it is not an absolute measure, but a judgement of relative worth. One distance learning package may cost 20 per cent more than another which covers the same topics. If that package is structured in such a way as to give the student greater autonomy in the way they approach their studies, with consequent higher satisfaction ratings and reports of greater confidence in their own learning abilities, then how might potential purchasers assess the cost effectiveness of those two packages?

Competitiveness

The requirement by funding agencies for providers to be competitive would be seen by some to be contentious. By competitive, I simply mean where education and training providers are judged against each other, rather than against some agreed goal. Commercial providers have long had to compete with other providers in the market place, but it is a relatively new experience for public sector providers – one of the results of cutbacks in funds or of new ways of allocating funds. In-house providers are also increasingly in the situation where they must compete with external providers.

Accountability

Being accountable, means making public what you are doing, or what you have done, for judgement by others. The publication of exam results, pass rates, recruitment figures, student numbers, etc, are simple examples of the kind of information which might be involved in this sort of exercise. In principle, accountability, or the taking of responsibility for what is or is not achieved, involves providing others with sufficient information to allow them to make their own judgements about the value or worth of that achievement.

Quality

There are a number of different ways of defining the term, but a consensus appears to be forming around the view of quality as 'fitness for purpose'. Richard Freeman (1991) suggests that using this view of quality in relation to open and distance learning materials would lead you to conclude that

- the product will superficially look 'right' but no more than that; there will be no sense of over-elaboration;
- that it will definitely work when put to the test;
- that it will definitely stand up to a cost-benefit analysis.

Accountability and evaluation

Who are you accountable to?

The extract which follows describes succinctly the problems for staff in public education and training organizations that the moves towards accountability present:

> I am accountable to my council as the governing body of this institute; to the Higher Education Funding Council – they give the money; to the DfE – they control teacher education; to the university – we are a constituent part of it; to auditors, internal and external – as accounting officer; to the Higher Education Quality Council – who review our quality assurance procedures; to HMI who judge the quality of our work; to those who provide funds for research because we have to assure them of the quality of what we do. And, somewhere along the line, I am also accountable to our customers – the students. (Peter Newsam, 1993)

You may care to reflect for a moment on the range of both internal and external bodies to whom you are accountable.

Realistically, evaluation must now take into account five different decision-making levels

- external funding, sponsoring or accrediting agencies;
- institutional level decision-makers;

- faculty/programme level decision-makers;
- course level decision-makers;
- students/customers.

The exercise of responsibility for open and distance teaching organizations by external agencies can require a variety of different forms of evaluation.

Figure 2.1 lists the main terms and methods used in evaluation for accountability and quality. Note the parallels in the distinction between the two terms quality control and quality assurance with the distinction between summative and formative evaluation which we saw in Chapter 1, the first being a judgement against an agreed standard, the second being an

Term	Purpose	Method
Quality Audit	assesses the quality assurance systems and procedures used by the organization	usually using peer review, internal or external audits can be carried out by either internal staff or external assessors as appropriate
Quality Assessment	assesses the teaching quality in specific subjects	uses both self assessment and external peer review
Accreditation	formal recognition by a recognized body that the level of provision is of an agreed standard	Normally uses both self-evaluation and on-site peer review
Quality Assurance	achieves defined standards through application of agreed procedures	can use range of formative evaluation approaches
Quality Control	rejection of products which fail to come up to a defined standard	can use a range of summative evaluation approaches
Self-Evaluation	externally or internally initiated self-critical review of achievements against specified goals	both formative and summative evaluation approaches may be used

Figure 2.1 *Terms and methods used in evaluation for accountability and quality*

identification of developmental needs in order to reach a specified standard.

The location of the responsibility for demonstrating quality of provision, and the design of the mechanisms for ensuring accountability is a sensitive area and one that can generate considerable anxiety and concern. Where the machinery of quality control is located outside organizations and when outcomes of quality assessment exercises are tied to funding decisions, considerable distrust can arise between those being assessed and those doing the assessing. Funders are dependent, however, on the organizations themselves for the evidence they need – for the information which will show clearly that investment in the provider provides good returns.

Monitoring and evaluation

Performance indicators

The question of how education and training provision should be judged has been been the subject of debate for some time. The problems start when it comes to specifying which activities should be included and the level of detail about them which is needed. To a considerable extent the information and type of analysis needed for judging the worth of a providers' activities will depend on who is making the judgement. Government bodies for instance are likely to be concerned about such issues as contributions to the labour market, or success in recruiting certain specified groups in the population. In contrast employers are likely to want evidence of skills acquired and competencies gained, while potential students may be more interested in the support available to students and the status of the qualifications gained. Funding agencies in the public sector are looking for evidence that their money has been well spent; in other words, that there is no waste of resources, and that society (or the particular part of it in which they have an interest) benefits from the activities of the providers in that sector.

The following extract is from a letter of guidance from the British Secretary of State to the Chairman of the former UK Polytechnics and Colleges Funding Council on the subject of accountability.

I shall however expect to see two key features. The first is a means of specifying clearly what [providers] are expected to provide in return for public funds. The second is a systematic method of monitoring institutional performance. I attach particular importance to the latter since, without measures of performance, the Council will have the means neither of satisfying itself that institutions are providing what has been promised at acceptable quality, nor of making comparative assessments of institutions as a basis for future allocations of grant. I look to the Council to develop further indicators of both the quality and the quantity of institutions' teaching and should be grateful if it would carefully consider how these might be used as an input to its funding policies and decisions. (Morris 1990)

The indicators to which he refers are performance indicators. These are 'statistics, ratios, costs and other forms of information which illuminate or measure progress in achieving the mission and the corresponding aims and objectives' (ibid). There is no doubt that there are considerable problems in describing institutional goals in such a way that they are measurable so that progress towards those goals can be accurately monitored. With the monitoring approach, no value judgements are required. The purpose of this type of approach is simply to provide a regular set of information from which any divergence from the situation expected could be identified. Such information would usually, but not necessarily, be of a quantitative nature.

Examples of the recommended indicators include application numbers, expenditure per student, progression and completion rates. Other indicators include measures of financial performance and what have been termed somewhat derisively as 'paperclip statistics'. Indicators of teaching performance continue to present us with problems. The danger is that indicators which are easy to identify will be collected rather than the ones which are relevant. Other dangers in using simple statistical indicators are their susceptibility to control, and the temptation of 'teaching to test', or working the system in order to score well on the selected indicators.

Quality measurement systems

Two quality measurement systems have received a great deal of attention, the British Standards Institution system (BS5750) and the Total Quality Management system (TQM), both of which formed the basis of the European pilot guide on quality for open and distance learning (SATURN 1992).

BS5750

The BS system and the International (ISO9000) and European (EN29000) series which are based on it are designed to enable manufacturers to produce goods to a measurable, controlled specification set by themselves. It does not guarantee the level of quality, merely its consistency. The costs of developing the detailed system and registering for recognition are high.

TQM

With TQM, the informing assumption is very much the formative one of continual quality improvement of the products and processes in order to meet customer requirements. It has been described as aiming to 'meet the customers' "defined" requirements at lowest cost, first time, every time' (Underwood 1991).

There is considerable pressure for evaluation to become an instrument of quality control, assessing the quality of the educational or training output before it reaches the students. At the same time, it is tempting for senior management to see evaluation as a quality assurance mechanism, providing the procedures necessary for the award and application of such quality assessment standards as BS5750. The limitations of such approaches to the maintenance and the improvement of quality in education and in open and distance learning have been well rehearsed (Calder 1992, Freeman 1991, Robinson 1992). As Halliday (1993) has pointed out:

> Application of the standard does *not assure quality*, only consistency. If the design or manufacturing standard is bad and results in an article of poor quality, BS5750 will help to ensure that further articles are made to a *consistently poor standard of quality*.

Nevertheless evaluation can make an important contribution in the development and maintenance of quality assurance systems without being limited, or confined, to those issues.

Self-evaluation

Self-evaluation is now a key part of the quality assessment exercise carried out by the UK Higher Education Funding Councils. It is also used extensively in other situations, such as for accreditation purposes, and as a synonym for evaluation for which responsibility lies with the unit that is the subject of the evaluation.

In Chapter 1, we discussed the idea of the learning organization. The examples we looked at concerned the identification of aspects of the teaching and learning systems which were not operating as intended. Two major writers on organizational learning, Chris Argyris and Donald Schön, have shown that we can look at organizational learning in the form of three types: single loop, double loop and deutero learning (Argyris and Schön 1978).

Single loop

This type of organizational learning is primarily concerned with achieving

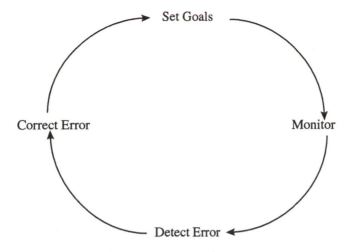

Figure 2.2 *Single loop learning*

existing goals and objectives. Findings from evaluation activities are used to correct errors in order to achieve the required standard of product or service. For example if the monitoring of the student demographic profile suggested that the targets for recruitment of students with lower qualifications were not being met, then reviews of the admissions procedures and possibly of marketing strategy might be undertaken. Changes to organizational strategies would be made in order to achieve the agreed target balance.

Double loop
In this type of organizational learning, the organization adapts by modifying its norms or assumptions. For example, if a provider of open and distance learning needed to grow in size in order to optimize its cost effectiveness, it might need to review the role which face-to-face provision played, or the type of support which was available to the student. Contradictions between different goals would be recognized and norms modified. Thus if targets for the amount of face-to-face support received by learners were not being met, the institution could respond in a variety of ways:

- it could cut back on its plans for growth in order to maintain the target levels of support (single loop learning);
- it might investigate alternative cheaper methods of personal support to students (double loop); or

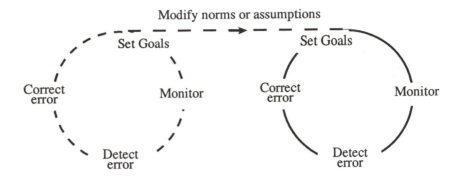

Figure 2.3 *Double loop learning*

- it might just redefine the target levels of support available to students (double loop).

Deutero learning
This form of organizational learning involves self-evaluation. By reflecting on past experience, identifying strengths and weaknesses in the way problems and errors are identified and solutions introduced, the organization learns how to become better at both single and double loop learning.

For example, suppose course evaluations are carried out by individual course teams. A self-evaluation might reveal that actions resulting from the student feedback are only implemented in a haphazard way. More effective action might occur if the timing of the evaluation was changed, or if the procedures for reporting on the utilization of evaluation findings were changed.

Conclusion

External demands for information from educational institutions have been increasing at a growing rate. The effect has been to throw into prominence the importance for institutions of having a coherent and coordinated programme evaluation and research capacity.

Organizational objectives now, more than possibly at any time in the past, need explicitly to include statements about the following:

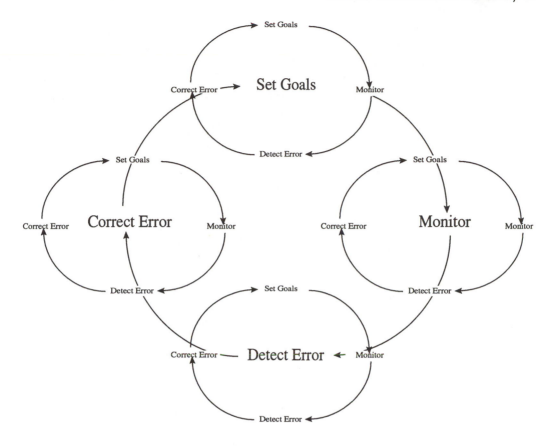

Figure 2.4 *Deutero learning*

- Attainment of certain minimum standards.
- Maintenance of quality of provision and service.
- Improvement of provision.

The effects of these diverse objectives on the nature of evaluation within organizations, and particularly in the field of open and distance learning, has still to be identified. Certainly programme evaluation can play an essential role in the cycle of both internal review and improvement and external reviews and audits.

An evaluation system therefore needs to take into account both internal and external demands for information. Many providers already have a considerable investment in evaluation and data collection. The most common problem is that it is rarely coordinated and systematized. The pressures with which educational institutions in particular have had to deal over the last few years has meant that evaluation activities have on the whole developed in an ad hoc fashion, to deal with the concerns of the moment. In the next chapter we will be looking at how data from student records can be used for evaluation purposes.

Chapter 3

Baseline student statistics

Usually one of the first questions anyone will ask in relation to the performance of a provider of open and distance learning is how many students they are catering for. The importance of the basic statistical information needed to answer such enquiries can easily be overlooked in the discussion and planning of programme evaluation needs. Providers of open and distance learning, both large and small, hold a valuable information resource in their student records. Because these are usually seen as administrative records, their potential as an evaluation tool can be easily overlooked.

The spread of the ideas of quality assurance and performance indicators into education is now leading providers to review just what data they do have which can be used for evaluation purposes. The challenge is to recognize the potential of administrative records for institutional research and evaluation. This chapter will discuss the types of data which can be collected as a matter of routine and the ways in which it can be used to underpin and illuminate other evaluation activities.

The need for information

Student statistics can reveal who the students are, where they come from, and what formal learning experience they bring with them. They can tell you how the student is progressing, at what stage in the course they may be experiencing difficulties, and whether they have given up. Finally they can indicate how well or badly the student has done. Changes in student progress and trends across different courses, different years and different presentations of a course can be monitored, giving early warning of areas of the system that may require further investigation. In other words, student statistics underpin all programme evaluation activities in open and distance teaching.

Consider the type of data which are recommended for use as performance indicators, and for institutional self-assessment shown in Figure 3.1. Although these are measures which are applied to universities in the UK, they are indicative of the kind of information which is increasingly expected of all public providers. Private or commercial providers will, on the whole, be similarly driven by the need for accountability and the need to compete with the public sector. What the figure shows clearly is the mix of different types of data, with statistical measures playing a particularly important part in the form of performance indicators. We now turn to examine some of the sources of those data which are often held by providers as a matter of routine.

Performance indicators	Institutional self assessment information	
	England	Scotland
• entry qualifications	• mission of the institution and published course documents	• aims and curricula
• applications		• curriculum design and review
• expenditure per student	• course aims, objectives and achievements	• teaching and learning environment
• progression and completion rates	• definition or under-standing of quality	• staff resources
• student attainment	• locus of responsibility for quality	• learning resources
• employment	• plans for maintaining and enhancing quality	• course organization
	• internal indicators of quality	• teaching and learning practice
		• student support
		• assessment and monitoring
		• students' work
		• output, outcomes and quality control

Figure 3.1 *Data used for the quality assessment of UK universities*
Source: Quality Support Centre 1992

Data resources

It often seems to be the case that providers of open and distance learning (and of other forms of learning as well) will say that they have no data on their students, or that they cannot afford to carry out any formal research. However, certain basic information about students has to be held by any open and distance learning unit or institution simply in order for it to function effectively.

Sources of data

Regardless of the major components of the teaching package, whether video, computer link-ups, audio conference or print, students must either be sent the material, or be sent details and updates of where and when the materials or the channels of communication can be accessed. Thus the absolute minimum information kept for each student would be their name and address or contact point and the name of the course for which they were registered. If students were company employees who had been referred to an in-company open and distance learning course, then their department, job title and work location would probably also be known. The student's sponsor and the fee they had been charged would be noted, as would details of any assessment results and exam results.

In other words there is always a basic set of data about students gathered and kept by providers. The problem is that they are kept by the providing organization for different purposes, and may be held by various sectors of the organization using various data category definitions and different data updating and control procedures. The data may also be held in a variety of formats on different computer or manual systems. Although the problems such situations can present are considerable, they are not insuperable.

Possible sources include data held on

- course registration records
- student fee payment records
- tutor fee payment records
- assignment records
- exam registration records

about individual

- enquirers
- applicants
- those offered a place

- those who have accepted a place
- current students
- past students

and so on.

One approach which is increasingly feasible through upgrades in computer capacity is to set up a research data-base (see Woodley and Ashby 1993, and Abbott-Chapman 1992). Copies of records from a variety of sources are brought together, set up and held in a form which enables research users to draw on and use the full range of student-based and course-based data held by the provider. The key link between all the files is the student's ID number. Data-standards have to be agreed, conformity with Data Protection Act requirements cleared, availability and accessibility of the data for use for evaluation purposes decided, procedures for protecting the confidentiality of individual data files agreed, together with the time periods covered by the statistics and responsibility for their updating and dissemination. All these issues have to be discussed and agreed.

Demographic data	Measures	Applications
Enrolment status	Total enrolments Enrolment trends	Measure of demand
Course choice	Trend data Subject/topic preferences	Effectiveness of marketing policy; equal opportunities policy
Geographic location	Dispersion and distribution of students	Distribution of materials; planning of student support; recruitment of staff
Fee income	Sponsorship levels	
Gender	Gender balance	
Age	Age profile	
Languages spoken	First and second languages	Course and programme evaluation studies, such as access, recruitment, retention, progress and success
Ethnic origin	Profiles of ethnic groups	
Place of work	Location distribution	
Highest educational level	Formal starting standard	

Figure 3.2 *Student demographics and utilization*

Basic evaluation measures

Figure 3.2 shows a checklist of student demographic data which can be used to provide different sorts of evaluation measures. The section above the dotted line shows the type of primary or basic data which all providers will hold.

Enrolment status

The size of the enrolment is usually the first criterion for measuring the effectiveness of an open and distance learning provider. The extent to which the target numbers have been achieved or exceeded can be used both internally and externally as a measure of success. An extract from the annual report for Athabasca University, a Canadian distance teaching institution, is given in Figure 3.3. Care has been taken in interpreting even these simple figures; there is a need to distinguish between student registrations and course registrations because some students take more than one course.

Course choice

The enrolment figures for different courses for example can provide a simple indication of the relative demand for those courses. However, differences in the way in which courses have been publicized, differences in the target groups for the different courses and fees which vary between courses are all examples of possible explanations for variations in recruitment between courses. Enrolment figures for individual courses over

---

Registrations by Mode of Study 1987–88 to 1989–90

Mode	1987–88		1988–89		1989–90	
Home Study	12163	83.6%	12856	79.5%	13207	80.7%
NIC*	720	4.9%	667	4.1%	500	3.1%
Seminar	1427	9.8%	2426	15.0%	2409	14.7%
Teleconference	236	1.6%	217	1.3%	249	1.5%

*North Island College

Pass Rates by Mode of Study 1987–88 to 1989–90

Year	Home Study	Seminar	Teleconference	NIC
1987–88	48.7	73.3	66.5	29.5
1988–89	51.6	78.5	66.8	32.9
1989–90	56.6	75.0	74.1	29.3

Figure 3.3 *Extract from Athabasca Annual Report showing annual student and course registrations.*

time displayed as trend data can also be very revealing. If the registrations for a particular course start to drop, comparisons with similar courses offered by the provider can be made to see if the problem is common to more than one course.

In the UK, the government recently decided to make available additional funds if certain organizations were able to achieve a specified increase in the number of maths, science and technology students. Data such as we have just been discussing would be essential evidence of meeting such recruitment targets.

Geographical dispersion

The addition of a geographical dimension through the analysis of students' addresses can provide key management data for marketing, course or student sponsorship and course design purposes. This data provides a measure with which to test the extent to which the provider is achieving their planned sphere of coverage – whether students are evenly dispersed within the area served by the provider, or the location of obvious imbalances. If the provider is supposed to be a national provider, but finds that 70 per cent of their students come from, say, the London area, then some review into the explanations for this imbalance can be undertaken. Similarly an in-house provider could find an imbalance in the take-up of courses by staff from different departments or from different work locations. The causes for the imbalance could then be the subject of further investigation.

Fee source

Information on the presence or absence of an official sponsor for course fees, and on the identity of that sponsor, can again be used for far more than the simple collection of payment by the financial arm of the organization.

An example is shown in Figure 3.4 of how this information can be used in conjunction with other data to show whether there is any difference in performance between students in receipt of different amounts of sponsorship. In the particular example shown, looking at the performance of recipients of Australian government grants in the University of Tasmania, there did not appear to be any difference (Abbott-Chapman et al 1992).

Gender mix

Gender information can be taken from people's titles, and is both an indicator of whether the providers' policy on gender mix and on equal opportunities is operating as planned. It can also show the gender balance for individual courses. For example, if the data show that courses on

Cumulative proportions by Austudy award

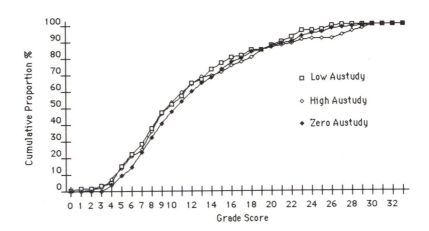

Cumulative totals by Austudy award

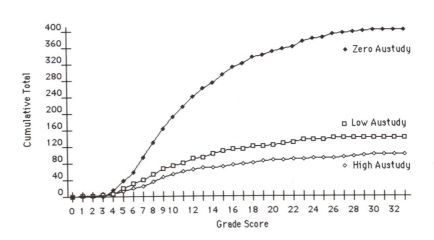

Figure 3.4 *Students grade scores analysed by amount of sponsorship received*
Source: Abbot-Chapman et al 1992, p 92

parenting and child-care are attracting mostly women, then either the recruitment and marketing strategy can take that fact into account, or action can be taken to try to attract more men. The action to be taken will depend on the policy of the organization.

Clearly there can be problems in the reliability of data such as this. For example, people may be registering for a course in order to acquire the materials and the 'registered student' of the course may not be the person or people who will be using the package of open learning materials. Nevertheless these data can still provide a useful range of planning and evaluation information.

With computerized address files for students, there is no reason why even the smallest provider cannot set up and maintain its own monitoring system for student statistics. Even when the data are at their most limited, a great deal of management information can be drawn from them. We will be examining some of the possibilities in the sections which follow.

Additional student demographic data

The demographics below the dotted line in Figure 3.2 comprise those which may need collecting as extra information from applicants. In practice, providers are often able to gather some of this information as a matter of routine. Additional data such as date of birth or age, educational qualifications held, occupation and ethnic group membership can lead not only to much more detailed descriptions of who the new students are and whether new groups are being recruited, but can also give a much better idea of the balance between different groups for the whole student body.

Uses of demographic data

For example, OU student demographic data showed early on that teachers formed a substantial percentage of the total student body – 41 per cent in 1971 (see Figure 3.5). However, as the 'backlog' of older non-graduate teachers was dealt with over a number of years, the importance of that occupational group in terms of size declined to only 8 per cent in 1988, with a consequent reduction in the demand for certain courses.

Demographic statistics are also necessary to examine relationships between the student 'input' and their subsequent progress. For example, younger students have been found to be at greater risk of not completing their courses (Woodley and McIntosh 1980). Similarly, the comparative success of students from different regions, or on different courses can be monitored (see Ashby 1992 for an example of this type of analysis). Analyses

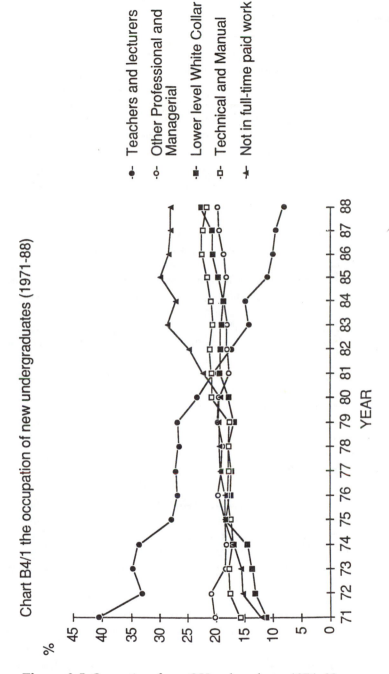

Figure 3.5 *Occupation of new OU undergraduates 1971–88*
Source: Open University Equal Opportunities Statistical Digest. April 1990, Chart B4/1

of the progress of these particular groups might suggest whether there was a need to provide extra support or counselling at an early stage.

Here the data would both provide indicators of the provider's effectiveness in reaching recruitment targets (such as the unemployed, or younger people, or members of ethnic minorities) for courses, programmes or for the institution overall, as well as for planning purposes in relation to support needs.

The rationale for the collection and analysis of these basic statistics must include the different types of problem which they can inform. At the course level, course designers have to make certain assumptions about the type of person who will register for their course. It may be that they are expected to be a practising teacher, or a relatively experienced manager. Students may be expected to bring certain levels of competence in core study skills or discipline areas.

For example, if the assignment work in a course for middle managers is based on the assumption that the students will have access to certain kinds of information at work and this is not in fact the case, then there will be immediate problems for both the students and the course designers with respect to the assessment. If the students who actually register for the course do not match the profile expected by the course designers, then this may explain lack of satisfactory progress with the course. It also raises questions about how such students came to be recruited to the course, whether the details of the course requirements given to students were accurate and whether modifications either to the recruitment procedure or to the course need to be made.

Collection of student demographic data

The question of where this additional information comes from is an important one. If the provider prefers to recruit students through such methods as the 'cut out coupon' which accompanies the fee payment, then the additional data must come from a separate data collection exercise. The opposite extreme is the five-page application form full of detailed questions which can be used to confirm the fulfilment of entry requirements, but which are so often underutilized for subsequent monitoring.

If the collection of student demographic data is carried out as a separate exercise from the actual registration on or purchase of a course, then it is highly likely that the data will be incomplete as not everyone will complete and return a separate form. It will also be more expensive to collect and to update. Really the issue has to be seen as a trade off among

- a simple single stage collection of very limited data,
- a two-stage collection of data, using a simple first stage, but accepting

that data will be not be forthcoming from all students at the second stage; and

- a single-stage collection of more extended data with a set of basic demographic data for teaching and planning purposes, but with the drawback of having to get the form to the applicant and completed by them without losing them in the process.

Where can I do the course?

You do not have to go anywhere to do this course. You can do it in your own time, wherever and whenever you can. You can start the course at any time. Study on your own or with a friend

You may choose to ask an organisation to sponsor you.

How do I enrol on the course?

Just fill in the form below and send it off to the address shown.

— — — — — — — — — — — — ✂ — — — — — — — — — — — — —

To : WEA - 6 Brewer Street, Oxford OX1 1QN

Name : ....

Address : ....

....Tel...........................

Please enrol me on **Focus on France/Focus on Germany** (delete which is not applicable).

I enclose my fee of £ 35.00 made payable to **WEA Thames and Solent**

Figure 3.6 *Sample application forms/questions*
Source: NEA Thames and Solart, 1993

Read the instructions on the front of this form and the information in *Becoming a student*. Then refer to 'How to complete Application Form LAC/01' as you answer each question. Questions with a box round them are compulsory; all the others are optional.

PERSONAL DETAILS

1 Surname/family name

2 First names in full

3 Mr/Mrs/Ms etc.   Initials

4 Date of birth   Please give this in numbers, e.g. 09 08 34

Day   Month   Year

In order to apply you must be 18 or over on 1 January 1993

5 Are you (please tick)

Male   Female

6 The address you want us to put on any correspondence to you

7 Postcode (UK residents only)

8 Telephone number (with STD code)

Day   Ext.

Evening   Ext.

9 May we release your name, address and telephone number to other students to set up study groups?

Yes   No

Address

Day telephone number

Evening telephone number

10 Have you applied to study any of our courses before?

No   Yes   Your personal identifier (if you know it)

11 Enter the codes from Table 1 of *Becoming a student* for the study centre most convenient for you and its region.

Study centre   Region

12 Enter the code from Table 5 that best indicates your highest level of education.

13a Enter the code from Table 3 that best describes your present situation.

Code 1   Code 2

13b Which code from Table 4 best describes your present occupation, and what is your job?

Code   Your job

14 Enter the code from Table 2 that you feel most nearly fits your ethnic origin.

15 Some courses include home computing. Please tick the disk size you will want.

3.5" disks   5.25" disks

Please tick *one* box. If your machine takes both, you will want the size for drive A.

16 Where do you expect to be living from 1 January 1993?

United Kingdom, Republic of Ireland or any other EC country

Any other country

If not in the United Kingdom, which country will you be living in?

Figure 3.6 *cont.*
Source: Open University, 1993.

Student progress and drop-out

After registering for a course, the study career of a student can take many routes. They may never actually start their studies or their training, or they may start but be unable for some reason to complete the course. Such students may withdraw or, more often, they may just not turn up to tutorials, or submit assignments. Some students may continue to the end of their course, but either not complete all the assignments or fail to reach the standard needed to successfully complete the course. Those who are successful may go straight on to the next course if they are seeking some qualification which is based on a series of courses, or they may take a break and continue later; they may transfer to another institution, or they may just end their studies.

Problems when monitoring student progress

As education and training provision becomes more flexible, the lines between active and inactive students become increasingly blurred. The use of flowcharts to show the progress of groups of students is now widespread. The movement of students from point of entry to completion of the qualification or the programme of study for which they have registered shows clearly the points at which greatest student losses occur.

The monitoring of students as they enter the system presents relatively few problems. However, general understanding of the need not only to recruit people but also to provide effective and efficient provision for them once they have been recruited is still growing. The danger of the 'revolving door' syndrome where the increased opportunity to start studies or training is unfortunately matched by the opportunity to drop-out or fail was first identified in the USA at the time when positive discrimination was being introduced into higher education (see Cope and Hannah 1975). The challenge is to identify the potential trouble spots which might impede students' progress or lead to their dropping out of the course. Suitable modifications to the course materials or to the systems or procedures presenting the problem can then be made.

In addition to the question of the organization's responsibility to its students are issues of planning and production of course materials in relation to student numbers. Costs of course materials production and distribution, tutorial support, student assessment and examinations are all dependent on student numbers. The more accurate the estimates of future student numbers, the less waste there will be in the system. At the same time, the question of student commitment to certain lines of study is important. The

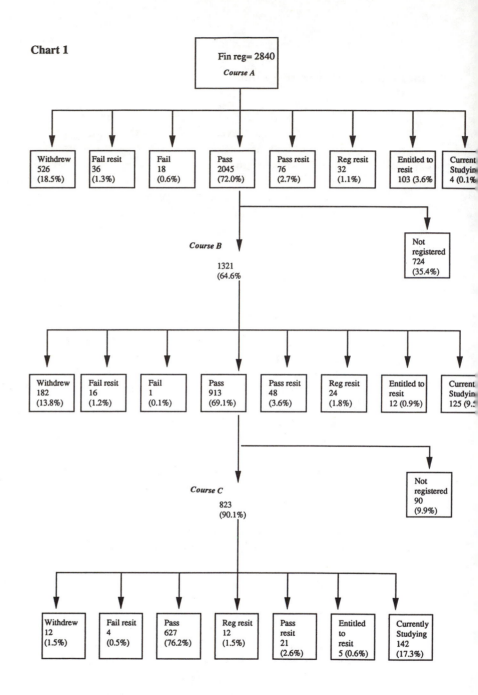

Figure 3.7 *Flowchart showing main stages of student progress*
Source: Ashby 1992

number of students moving through on to more advanced courses can make the difference between the viability or otherwise of advanced courses.

Student progress at the course level

How do we keep track of the students once they have registered for a course? Much has been written about the great variations in the design and structure of open and distance learning courses and systems. They can vary from very rigid and traditional provision based on live broadcasts which are studied by groups of students on multiple sites, such as the CRTVU (Central Radio and Television University) in China provides, through to very flexible provision where the students in effect structure their own study and fit in with the institutional timetable only for assessment purposes as with the Indira Gandhi Open University in India.

This can mean that even relatively simple pieces of information such as the length of time the students take to complete a course and the proportion of them who do so successfully is not known until the time limits (if there are any) expire. Figure 3.8 shows three ways of students moving through a system. In (i) a measurement or a collection of data is taken at the point of entry; students can then take varying amounts of time to complete their course (or in some cases, never to complete). In (ii) the measurement or the collection of data takes place at the point of official exit. This approach will not pick up those who have dropped out along the way. In (iii) measurements which take place at both entry and exit can be taken with all students expected to study at the same pace. A clearer picture of the loss of students along the way can be drawn with this approach, but this is only possible where there is a common fixed period of study.

Such problems are important because measures such as pass rates, and non-completion rates are crucial to providers both for internal evaluation of their teaching and other systems, and also as external performance indicators. Notice that I use the term non-completion. A great deal has been written on student drop-out. For courses or programmes of study which involve regular milestones such as assessments which students have to complete over set periods of time, the identification of students who are failing to meet the requirements for progress through the course or through the programme of study can be relatively easily identified. However, for providers who allow students flexibility in respect of the speed at which they study, or time in which to complete assignments, then the only way they can find out whether students still regard themselves as active or not is to contact them and ask them. This is usually done by means of a survey.

Let us consider the issue of student progress through a particular course.

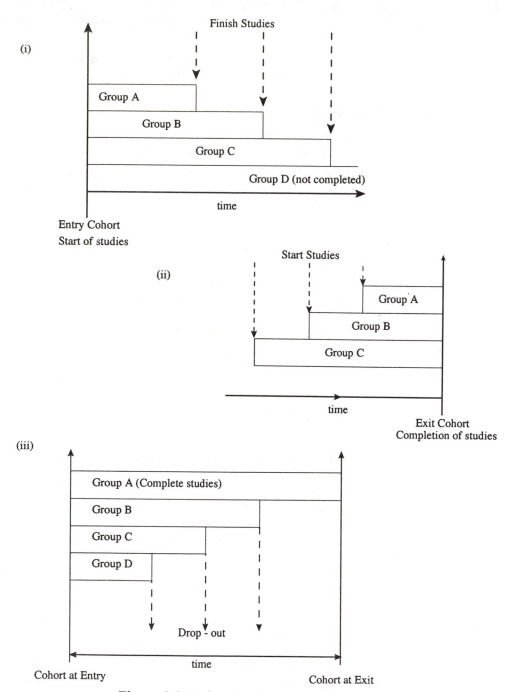

Figure 3.8 *Student throughput and points of measurement*

The worst case from a monitoring point of view would be a situation where the student registered, was provided with the course materials or components, and then only had to appear for an exam at a date which they were able to select from a choice of several. Until the student registered their intention to sit the exam, the provider would have no way of knowing whether that student had even started the course. In such situations the provider would have no alternative way of monitoring students' progress other than by special monitoring studies.

The situation the provider would be in would resemble Figure 3.8 (i). In other words, for any cohort of students, some would be progressing well and would register their intent to take the exam or for recognition of completion of their course at the earliest possible point (Group A), some would be progressing but at slower speeds or with gaps in their studies, and would register for their exam at later points (Groups B and C), and some students would fail to emerge at all (Group D). It is this last group which can present so many problems for providers. Are they actually still studying, albeit very slowly, or are they 'resting' but intending to return to their studies at some point in the future, or have they, for whatever reason, given up any intention of completing their studies?

The existence of these different groups is one of the reasons why it can be so difficult for a provider of open and distance learning to give a sensible or accurate answer to the question of the level of student drop-out from their courses. In the sort of context where the attendance and work requirements of the course are extremely flexible, the question of whether a student has dropped out is unlikely to be determined by their failure to conform to those requirements, but rather by the personal intentions of that student.

Milestones of progress through a course

Usually, however, some form of 'milestones' in the form of intermediate data on students at points between registration and final exam are available. For example, attendance at tutorial or counselling sessions could be monitored, or submission of assignments for assessment would give a substantial amount of information on the progress of students.

Figure 3.9(a) shows how the progress of two students can look from their assessment records. Each has to submit three assignments out of a number spread throughout the period of the course. Student A submits nothing until towards the middle of the course when three are submitted in quick succession. There is then no further assessment contact until the final exam. Student B has a rather different pattern of submission, with one very

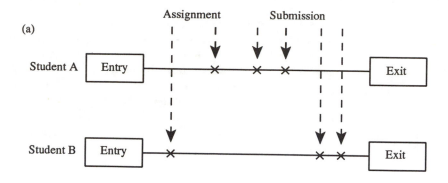

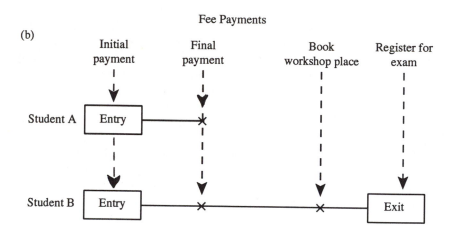

Figure 3.9 *Using milestones to monitor student progress*

early on and nothing else until the very last minute. Again, there is no way of telling from the assessment data alone whether or not this student was still studying until almost the end of the course.

Assessment data can be used in three rather different ways. The first way is to analyse the data in aggregate in order to improve the course. For example, the marks achieved on the different assignments and the varying popularity of the different assignments could indicate those areas of the course with which students had problems. The second way would be to identify particular groups of students who appeared from the assignment data to be having difficulties. This would involve using any student demographic data which was held on students and merging it with the assessment data. Both these uses of the data involve retrospective or after-the-event analysis for formative purposes. The third way in which assessment records can be used is to monitor the individual progress of students. Any lack of activity beyond a specified period could then trigger enquiries of the student as to whether they needed any additional support or help.

Figure 3.9(b) shows a set of fixed administrative milestones using a fee-payment system, as they might apply to the same two students. Both students pay their initial fee and their final payment by the due date. However, when it comes to the next milestone of, say, registering for a site visit, or for a weekend school, only student B is still active. So administrative records such as fee payment data can be used to give additional information about the progress of individual students. We can now tell that student A ceased to participate actively in the course at some point between the payment of the final stage of the course fee and the deadline for booking a place for the weekend school.

Figure 3.10 shows an extract from the information to course teams at the Open University which brings together data from different sources for regular updates on how students are progressing through the course. From this data the course designers can see at what point the course appears to be losing students, while changes in the student demographic profile identify which groups of students are being lost.

Student outcomes

The exam is usually the final course milestone for students. There are two sets of exam data which can help in illuminating how the students have progressed. The first relates to the students who actually get as far as sitting the exam, while the second is the actual exam results. For example, an exam pass rate of 95 per cent might look rather good unless you also knew that the proportion of students who actually got as far as sitting the exam was only 55 per cent of those originally registered. Similarly an exam pass rate of 40 per cent might look pretty dreadful unless you were also aware that 90 per cent of those who started the course had continued as far as the exam. (In practice such a low pass rate for students motivated enough to have got so far with the course would give cause for concern.) Exam data is as useful as all the other student milestone data for identifying areas of concern, for monitoring student progress and, just as importantly, for using with demographic data to identify weaknesses in the courses and to anticipate future students who may have special needs.

```
                                 06/04/93
                                 KCA05/86                              The Open University Management
                            Analysis milestone : 23/03/93 - Fi    Survey Research Department's Course-based Analysis
                            Baseline milestone : r.                          Registration - continuing
                            Baseline d-+                                     -----------------------------
        06/04/93                        The Open University Management Serv 01/01/93
        KCA05/86        Survey Research Department's Course-based Analysis of 01/01/93
        Analysis milestone : 23/03/93 - Final Registration - continuing stuones
        Baseline milestone : Initial Reg/Alloc ----------------------------us year-! Students who
        Baseline dates - continuing students : 01/01/93                     %PR %FR ! submitted
                          new students : 01/01/93                                    ! specific TMAS
                                                                        76 100 ! TMA   -----------
          OU Region     No. V% %In  ! Present occupation  No. V% %In  ! 00 131 !
          ---------                 ! ------------------               ! 76 100 !      No. V% %In
          London        48 14  75   ! Housewives - at home 67 20  78  ! '3  96 ! 01    70 20 100
          South         24  7  71   !            - pt work 24  7  92  ! R   89 ! 02     0  0   0
          South West    29  8  79   ! Armed Forces          4  1 100  ! 8   76 ! 03     0  0   0
          W. Midlands   25  7  84   ! Admin. & Managerial  18  5  78  ! 6   72 ! 04     0  0   0
          E. Midlands   24  7  67   ! Teachers - primary    5  1 100  ! -----  ! 05     0  0   0
          East Anglia   41 12  90   !          - secondary  8  2 100  !        ! 06     0  0   0
          Yorkshire     18  5  94   !          - higher ed  2  1  50  ! %In    ! 07     0  0   0 !
          North West    24  7  63   !          - other      2  1 100  !        ! 08     0  0   0 !
          North         11  3  73   ! Medical professions  13  4  77  ! 78     ! 09     0  0   0 !
          Wales         12  3  83   ! Social Services       4  1  50  ! 50     ! 10     0  0   0 !
          Scotland      39 11  87   ! Other profs. & Arts  26  8  85  ! 71     ! 11     0  0   0 !
          N. Ireland     8  2  88   ! Qual. science & eng.  9  3  89  ! 100    ! 12     0  0   0 !
          South East    40 12  75   ! Technical personnel  11  3  91  ! 86     ! 13     0  0   0 !
          No data        0  0   0   ! Skilled trades        6  2  83  ! 67     ! 14     0  0   0 !
                                    ! Other manual work     4  1  75  ! 91     !
          Sex           No. V% %In  ! Communics & transpt   2  1 100  ! 0      !
          ---                       ! Clerical & office    83 24  70  ! )0     !
          Male         114 33  75   ! Sales & services     20  6  70  !        !
          Female       229 67  81   ! Retired              31  9  81  !        ! Students who
          No data        0  0   0   ! In Institutions       3  1 100  !        ! submitted
                                    ! No data               1  0 100  !        ! specific CMAS
          Year of Birth             !                                          ! ----------------
          -------------             !                                          ! CMA No. V% %In
          Before 1911    0  0   0   !                                          ! 41    0  0   0
          1911 - 1915    1  0 100   !                                          ! 42    0  0   0
          1916 - 1920    5  1  80   ! Occupation on entry No. V% %In           ! 43    0  0   0 !
          1921 - 1925   13  4 100   ! ------------------                       ! 44    0  0   0 !
          1926 - 1930   22  6  82   ! Housewives - at home 71 21  79  !        ! 45    0  0   0 !
          1931 - 1935   13  4  77   !            - pt work 19  6  89  !        ! 46    0  0   0 !
          1936 - 1940   26  8  73   ! Armed Forces          5  1 100  !        ! 47    0  0   0 !
          1941 - 1945   49 14  80   ! Admin. & Managerial  15  4  80  !        ! 48    0  0   0 !
          1946 - 1950   54 16  78   ! Teachers - primary    4  1 100  !        ! 49    0  0   0 !
          1951 - 1955   66 19  71   !          - secondary  9  3 100  !        ! 50    0  0   0 !
          1956 - 1960   53 15  81   !          - higher ed  1  0   0  !        ! 51    0  0   0 !
          1961 - 1965   35 10  83   !          - other      2  1 100  !        ! 52    0  0   0 !
          1966 & after   6  2 100   ! Medical professions  15  4  80  !        ! 53    0  0   0 !
          No data        0  0   0   ! Social Services       3  1  67  !        ! 4     0  0   0 !
                                    ! Other profs. & Arts  29  8  76  !        ! 5     0  0   0 !
          Age ended F.t.            ! Qual. science & eng.  7  2  86  !        ! 6     0  0   0 !
          Education     No. V% %In  ! Technical personnel  12  3  92  !        ! 7     0  0   0 !
          ---------                 ! Skilled trades        7  2  71  !        !
          15 & under    32  9  81   ! Other manual work     4  1  75  !        !      0  0   0 !
          16            64 19  77   ! Communics & transpt   2  1 100  !        !      0  0   0 !
          17            53 15  77   ! Clerical & office    85 25  72  !        !      0  0   0 !
          18            56 16  82   ! Sales & services     20  6  70  !
          19            16  5  63   ! Retired              28  8  82  !
          20            19  6  74   ! In Institutions       3  1 100  !
          21 & over     50 15  78   ! No data               2  1 100  !
          No data       53 15  87   !
```

Figure 3.10 *Course-based student progress and profiles*
Source: Open University Management Services Division

Conclusion

Even though students may be successful in individual courses, students' progress from course to course and particularly the attrition rates between courses can present providers with considerable problems. Issues such as the rate of student throughput, the pathways they choose through the courses, the points at which they appear to become dormant and the periods for which they become dormant all impinge directly on such areas as planning activities associated with course numbers, information and publicity about courses and their marketing and recruitment strategies, the amount, type and timing of support offered to students, and on course improvement.

The limitation of student statistics is that they can be used to track down problem points, but for an explanation as to *why* there are problems, student feedback of some kind will need to be arranged. In the coming chapters we will be looking further at the use and potential of different methods of getting feedback and opinions from students and tutors.

Chapter 4

Programme and curriculum development

Introduction

Three key perspectives at the programme level are the range and type of courses which are provided, the viability of those courses and the quality of the total student experience. The next three chapters will be focusing on those questions as we examine the ways in which programme evaluation in open and distance learning can contribute to organizational decision-making. In this chapter we will be looking in detail at the ways in which evaluation can contribute to programme and curriculum development with respect to the range and types of courses provided and their viability.

Major issues at the programme level

It is at the programme level that major curriculum and course planning responsibilities usually lie. In this context, programmes refer to courses or open and distance learning packages which are organized and administered together by a provider because they have a common focus. This common focus may be type of qualification, the particular community being served, the form of funding, the teaching medium used, the subject matter, the level at which the courses are taught, or the structure of the course or package being offered to the learner. So, for example, you may have a distance teaching programme within an organization which also offers face-to-face teaching; or you may offer a programme of training for senior managers; or a programme of training in information technology. Whatever the focal theme is for your programme, policies and decisions on all these issues will need to be informed by findings gathered through programme evaluation activities.

Programme development

A programme needs to ensure as far as possible that the range of topics covered, the structure of the courses, their length, level, workload, teaching approach and format are what is needed and wanted by the potential students and other stakeholders. Those with a stake in the success of individual programmes can include

- the providing institution;
- the funding agency;
- employers;
- course developers;
- tutors and course support staff;
- students/trainees;
- potential students.

You may be able to add other stakeholders to this list in relation to programmes offered by your own institution.

Methods for identifying learning/training needs

Let us consider what methods are available for identifying learning and training needs. Different types of providers have developed a range of methods (see Figure 4.1).

Task group/working party
The task group/working party approach involves the gathering together of a small group of key people charged with the responsibility of drawing up some form of plan for the programme that will identify principles and

---

Task group representing the spectrum of interests

Consultation of experts, clients and target audiences

Quantitative analyses of knowledge/skill shortage areas

Monitoring and analysis of demand for existing courses

Studies of employers to identify current and anticipated training needs, existing students and potential students

---

Figure 4.1 *Methods for identifying learning/training needs*

policy. For example, a working group was the approach used by the Monash University College in Gippsland, Australia, after the college had been nominated as a Distance Education Centre. Over a six-month period, the working party produced a series of discussion and direction papers intended to provoke discussion and debate about the administration, course development procedures, delivery styles and activities which the centre would undertake in developing a programme of distance education courses (Moodie and Nation 1993).

Consultation with experts, clients and target audiences
The advantage of following the consultative route, particularly through workshops and conferences, is the high quality and quantity of the information about training needs and preferences which can be gathered. Enthusiastic supporters and key people for future help during the programme development and dissemination stages can also be identified. However the disadvantage is that the people who participate in such events may not be typical of the people whose views and opinions you seek.

Quantitative analyses
The usefulness of simple desk research should not be overlooked. The Director of the Open College, Sheila Innes (1989) comments 'The college also conducts desk research into national trends, other training opportunities, and many other developments that relate to the planning needs of the Open College.' The monitoring of knowledge and skill shortage areas is not a one-off task, but a continuing need, both to see where future demands are likely to occur, and to see what other providers are doing.

Monitoring and analysis of demand for existing courses
Registration trends over time as well as trends in student profiles can be monitored from your own statistical data-base. Chapter 3 discusses this topic in some detail.

Studies of employers, existing students and potential students
The type of study you choose will depend on what kind of information you want from them and the time and resources you have available to spend on them. Case studies, group discussions and surveys can be used. The surveys can be based on face-to-face interviews using a short structured questionnaire, although this is an expensive option. Telephone surveys are somewhat cheaper, while postal questionnaires are also a useful option, although response rates can present a problem.

An example – the UK Open Tech Programme

In the mid-eighties, the UK government funded and set up the Open Tech Programme. Their aim was to meet skills shortages by encouraging the development of training opportunities for adults through open learning. Adults who needed training were the target group, with the 'needs of high technology companies . . . and the needs of small businesses' being given a high priority (Tavistock 1987). Nearly 140 local projects were developed and funded as part of the programme:

> Our case studies suggest that projects setting out to develop innovative syllabi were often located in host institutions which, based on a number of years' collaboration with firms, had built up an analysis of the nature of the changes in the work of the target group and the training needs stemming from these. Such an analysis was at least as important as any data collected from employers specifically for the OTP project because it provided an overall framework or conception of the target group's training needs, which could be used for interpreting data collected empirically. (Ibid: 38)

The Tavistock reported that the projects in the Open Tech Programme used a number of methods for identifying training needs:

> Approximately half the delivery projects carried out some kind of formal survey of their own of employers in their region of operation. In addition, about one half used already existing studies of particular aspects of skill requirements at local or national level, or regional manpower projections. Apart from this, about 40 per cent of delivery projects used various informal contacts with local industry to assess needs. In the typical LEA delivery project comprising a network of colleges coordinated and serviced through a central unit, these informal contacts were commonly ones that had already been built up between employers and various college departments. In deciding what Open Learning provisions the network as a whole should offer, staff at the central unit consulted with college departments to gain an overall picture of need in the region. (Ibid: 35).

What this example shows us is how a mix of different methods can be used, as a form of triangulation, to cross check and reinforce conclusions about the needs of a specific target group – adults who needed training in the skills needed by small businesses and high technology companies.

What to ask in a needs assessment study

The sorts of issues which a needs assessment or curriculum development study might investigate would include:

- topics, themes, and areas of desired study;
- preferred timing, duration and intensity of study;
- study orientation;
- media availability and preferences;
- support needs and preferences;
- pedagogic needs (academic and study skills);
- competencies to be achieved;
- extent of commitment to the organization providing the courses or learning packages (and alternative sources of training considered).

17. Please indicate which one of the following most <u>interests</u> you in terms of gaining qualifications/training relevant to your employment

General engineering .... 1 *(78)*

Mechanics 2

Electronics 3

Materials 4

Systems 5

Design 6

Computer systems/programming 7

Other *(please write in)* 8

18. Which of the following represents your main concern in terms of your needs in the employment field?

Updating existing knowledge .... 1 *(79)*

Gaining new <u>practical</u> skills, (e.g. programming language, experience of micros, learning systems analysis techniques) 2

Enlarging my understanding of <u>technological concepts, theories, ideas</u>............. 3

Just getting an up-to-date <u>qualification</u> to show my motivation/ increase my confidence 4

Figure 4.2 *Sample questions: needs assessment study*
Source: Qns 17 and 18 from 'Needs of women technologists' study. Swift & Swarbrick 1983

For example, look at the two questions in Figure 4.2 These were part of a questionnaire used in a survey of the needs of women technologists who were eligible for a special UK government bursary scheme. These two questions were designed to find out the relative importance of major motivating factors and the extent of the demand for different specialist areas in the field of technology. This latter question would enable the evaluator to advise on what the potential students' concerns were so that they could be reflected in the course aims, or if that was not possible, at least addressed in the programme information received by enquirers.

The question relating to the extent of the demand for different specialist areas would contribute both to the development of a bursary scheme in appropriate topic areas and would also give some indication of the levels

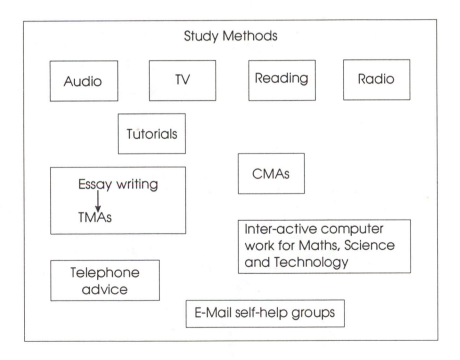

Figure 4.3 *Prompt board showing study components of potential open and distance learning packages*
Source: Durdle Davies distance learning packages 1993

of demand among the target group for courses in different specialist areas. In contrast, the question on the type of learning need would enable course developers to ensure that the needs of the target group were reflected in the focus of the course.

A rather different example is the group discussion approach. Figure 4.3 shows an example of the prompt board used by a market research company carrying out research into curriculum and course structure preferences for future open and distance learning packages.

The idea was to use the items on the board to help focus the discussion round the issue of component selection and media mix in future course packages. The issues which emerged from this activity could then be followed up in a quantitative study if it was felt necessary.

Programme viability

With both new and existing programmes, the question of viability has to be addressed (ie whether it can be developed and presented within the constraints set by the organization). Cost is usually one constraint, as is the question of student numbers. For a new programme, the aim may be to minimize costs for a set number of students, or to maximize student numbers for a set cost.

Options for research into programme viability

The options for assessing programme viability will to a certain extent depend on the strategic approach being adopted by the programme developers. Think about the situation where staff in your organization may be asking what sort of courses they should be thinking about developing for the future. Their traditional customer bases seem to be shrinking and the feeling is that they need to start thinking about something with wider appeal. Where would you start?

As the evaluation adviser for a study on programme development, you might want to know:

- Who their likely target groups were – is your organization thinking of extending the current group, getting a greater share of the 'market', or considering moving into totally new fields?
- What sort of topic areas are appropriate – again, an extension of a current range of courses, or a move into an area not previously offered by the organization?

You might also want to know:

- Who are their traditional customers.
- What pattern of study their students normally follow.
- What information they have about the motivation of their current students.
- What the conversion rate is from initial enquirers to signed-up students.

The exact questions on the list will vary depending on the context in which you are working. If you are dealing with in-company training, your questions would be somewhat different than if dealing with a local college open learning centre for example. Nevertheless the general approach would be the same in any situation.

The strategic options available to the programme developers are summarized in Figure 4.4.

Extension of provision to new target groups

The major problem with moving into provision for new target groups (cells 3 and 4) is in making contact with them in order to research their views and the likelihood of take-up of existing and new courses. For example, if you were thinking of extending your current range of courses, but wanted to aim for an entirely new target group such as farmers for instance, then you might think of approaching farmers' representatives and any associations whose membership included a high proportion of farmers as well as farmers

	Target Groups	
Topic areas	More of the same	New
More of the same	1	3
New	2	4

Figure 4.4 *Summary of major options for which different research strategies would have to be devised.*

themselves. The reason for this apparent 'overkill' approach is threefold:

- The proportion of farmers who will be seriously interested in the courses you have to offer is likely to be very small. Their response to a market research study is therefore likely to be quite low.
- The courses may be of interest to people in associated professions, belonging to the same organizations.
- You may be able to link up in some way with professional associations, either in the development of the courses, in the support you provide for students taking the courses, or in the marketing of the courses.

Expanding take-up by existing target groups

Suppose you are facing the situation (cells 1 and 2) where the aim is to increase take-up either by an increase in recruitment levels from your current target groups for current courses (more of the same), or by extending the current range of courses by introducing new areas. Think of the people whose opinion you would want to seek:

- existing students;
- former students;
- enquirers who had not gone ahead with their application;
- potential new clients.

Existing students
You would want to survey the opinions of existing students because they are among the most likely to be interested in the new courses. If they are currently studying with you, then they are familiar with the mode of study and the format. They also know the organization and the way it operates.

Former students
There is a similar situation with former students. There may be a number of reasons for the fact that they are former rather than current students. For example they may have been interested in continuing their studies, but the course choice wasn't to their liking; or they may simply have finished the particular course they were on and just not got round to registering for another. Whatever the reason, again, former students are familiar with the system and, if they are satisfied with their previous experiences of study with you, will be potentially interested in more courses from the same source.

Enquirers
People who have not gone ahead with their applications can be an important group to follow-up on. These are people who have heard about

your organization or your courses and have been sufficiently interested to get as far as finding out just what it is you have to offer. These are a potentially very important group in that if the courses which they would like to see provided match those which you are considering offering, the likelihood of take-up would be quite high.

We now consider an example of a study which focused on a specific target group with the aim of increasing take-up of training by the members of that group.

The SCOPME project

The UK Standing Committee On Postgraduate Medical Education (SCOPME) commissioned the Joint Centre for Education in Medicine to undertake qualitative research looking into a number of questions about the uptake of available provision by junior doctors in training grades. The aims of the study were to:

identify the incentives that encourage formal educational opportunities to be taken up and the barriers that prevent this. In more detail the aims were:

1 to describe and classify all types of formal postgraduate educational provision in selected specialities of hospital medicine at local, regional and national levels;
2 to identify incentives to participation in formal postgraduate training provision;
3 to identify barriers to participation in formal training;
4 to compare views of potential recipients/participants, facilitators, gatekeepers (ie those who give or withhold encouragement or permission to attend) and providers;
5 to devise strategies for influencing the type and amount of formal educational activity undertaken, including guidelines to providers for the design and presentation of courses;
6 to describe the role of the postgraduate dean in allocating funding for formal postgraduate training.

On this basis, strategies can be devised to enhance the accessibility and effectiveness of formal educational opportunities for doctors in the training grades . . . (Grant et al 1992)

As the aims show, both the reasons for lack of uptake as well as possible new areas and new forms of provision were investigated in this study. In other

STAGE	METHODS	OUTPUT
1 Classification and analysis of formal provision.	Documentary search. Interviews with providers.	Classification and analysis of types of provision.
2 Incentives and barriers to uptake.	Nominal group process. Juniors and seniors in medicine and surgery.	Force field analysis. Comparisons. Effects of variables.
3 Future strategies. Providers' guidelines.	Analysis of Stage 1 and Stage 2 findings.	Strategies for future action. Guidelines for providers.

Figure 4.5 *The SCOPME research design*
Source: Grant 1992, p 4

words, the concerns about the uptake of training opportunities by a specific target group led to research that would enable more effective marketing, more effective course presentation strategies and, if necessary, more appropriate forms of provision to meet the needs of that particular group.

The in-depth research design drew on a relatively small number of participants. Figure 4.5 shows that three research stages were used, combining three different qualitative techniques in order to explore and understand the views and experiences of the participants.

Piloting and pump-priming

The final stage in the programme development cycle is establishing whether or not the programme is capable of independent existence. The new or revised programme needs to be able to attract and retain enough students and sponsors willing to pay for or fund the programme at a level high enough to keep it going on a continuing basis.

So how do we go about getting the information which will enable the judgements about the viability of the programme to take place? Two approaches which are commonly used are pilot projects and pump-priming. A pilot is the initial trial of a method, approach or system prior to or as the first step towards its full-scale adoption. Pump-priming on the other hand is the time-limited initial subsidy of a new development in order to facilitate its diffusion and wider adoption. The Open Tech Programme we looked at earlier is an example of the pump-priming approach.

Pump-priming by the Open Tech

One of the primary aims of the UK Open Tech Programme was the dissemination of materials and of open learning ideas through local projects which were intended to survive as long as possible. The pump-priming emphasis was reflected in the focus on formative evaluation. An interesting aspect of this particular programme was the two-level nature of the evaluation, with each individual project being expected to carry out self-evaluation while the programme level evaluation focused on programme-wide issues, albeit still through a formative approach.

Funding of projects was to be on a short-term 'pump-priming' basis. The TGR [Task Group Report] expected employers and individuals to be willing to pay for projects 'really meeting a labour market need'.

It was intended from the outset of the Open Tech Programme that there should be an 'objective evaluation' of OTP. The Task Group Report recognized that within the timescale of four years 'many longer term outcomes will not be measurable'. The TGR considered it essential however 'that a periodic and cumulative review is made during this period, so that informed longer-term decisions can be made on the future use of the OTP after the first four years and that the experience of the initial phase is fully made use of in future arrangements'. (TGR: 13)

The evaluation was intended to cover projects and the Programme as a whole. 'Self-Evaluation' was seen as an important vehicle for project level evaluation. The adequacy of such self-evaluation was even intended to be one of the 'criteria for approving projects'. Programme-level evaluation was partly to be 'built on individual project evaluations' but was also to include the 'effectiveness and efficiency of the management of the programme' and 'the way the education and training system as a whole has responded, collaborated and adapted' and included other Programme-level considerations such as information, quality, staff development, and other programme outputs.

It was in March 1983, nine months after the Task Group reported, that the invitation to tender for this evaluation was circulated by

MSC; appropriately enough in a project-based Programme, the evaluation was also to be contracted out. By this time the evaluation had been re-labelled a 'development review', partly because it was thought important by the MSC that this activity should make a positive contribution to the Programme's development while it was still underway, by providing feedback and informing Programme management decisions. The change in the label also indicated some unease within the recently-established OTU [Open Tech Unit] about the idea of an independent evaluation. The Development Review (DR) was eventually commissioned in October 1983. (Tavistock 1987)

Piloting a new approach at British Telecom

For an example of a pilot, we now look at a major programme of company-based training courses using interactive video packs which was introduced at British Telecom. It was evaluated in order to inform decisions about future courses. The evaluator reported that:

The production of interactive videos and associated learning materials is the responsibility of the Distance Learning Section . . . within British Telecom's central Training Department. The Unit wanted to determine how effective the Appraisal and Counselling course had been as part of the management training programme, but the focus of any evaluation study would be the distance learning delivery package (interactive video [IV] plus workshop) to a greater extent than the Appraisal and Counselling course *per se*. It was never intended that the proposed 'summative' evaluation project would lead to significant modifications being made to the course; it would be too expensive to make changes to the IV at that stage. Instead, the project aimed to provide information about the course 'in action', with findings being used to inform the design, production and presentation of subsequent IV training courses.

The launch of the [IV] . . . training package coincided with the expansion in the activities of many district training departments. In fact, the course was developed partly in response to requests from district training departments who were finding it difficult to provide the necessary volume of training in appraisal and counselling by traditional methods . . .

The Appraisal and Counselling course appears to have been well received by managers and trainers. Furthermore, both groups were enthusiastic about the combination of IV and workshop as a method of training. The findings of this evaluation study corroborate the available research results in respect of IV, as reviewed recently: 'Interactive video is well-liked by users and achieves high levels of learner success. It achieves significant cost benefits for applications involving a large requirement for distributed training and it compresses the time usually required for training' (Copeland, 1988). (Kirkwood 1992)

Judgements about viability

Would either of these approaches enable the decision-makers to make judgements about the viability of their programmes? For the British Telecom pilot study, the mix of summative and formative evaluation produced clear positive conclusions:.

> The evaluation of the centrally organized, but locally tested project clearly provided sufficient and appropriate information both for deciding on the viability of the new approach and for informing the development of the programme which was to follow. (Kirkwood 1992)

As another writer pointed out in discussing this scheme, 'At an estimated saving of £300 per student [1990 prices] the direct savings [to the company] resulting from the course are likely to amount to £8 million' (Brown 1990).

In contrast, the evaluation of the pump-priming programme represented by the Open Tech Development Review resulted in less clear-cut outcomes. The decision to discontinue the project was taken some three months before the evaluation report was due. However it is clear that the decision to go for a primarily formative approach which emphasized self-evaluation did mean that local projects had benefited as much as they could have done from the evaluation work, and were in a much improved position for continuing as independent projects. The final test of viability could be said to be the 'sink or swim' approach. As Nigel Paine pointed out in his review of the evaluation report:

> Many of its lessons have been absorbed, directly or indirectly, by the organizations and programmes which have continued beyond the Open Tech Programme and those organizations, particularly the Open College, which were set up in its wake. Undoubtedly the Open Tech Programme was not completely successful, but this report also demonstrates forcibly that it was by no means a failure. The legacy of expertise gained through the Open Tech Programme is still fuelling

many open learning developments today and most of the key, corporate players in the open learning field cut their teeth on the Open Tech. (Paine, 1990)

Conclusion

A minimum level of demand is essential to sustain the initial investment and the setting up of support for or development of any open learning or distance taught course. Even where the determining criterion is national need or academic desirability the providing organization will still need to carry out some basic formal research studies for new courses and programmes. The strategic questions in such instances will be whether sufficient demand can be generated for the proposed programme of courses and whether student motivation can be sustained over the length of their studies. The particular needs to be met by the courses within the programme in terms of knowledge, skills and competences will need to be determined, and the academic and professional rigour of the particular syllabus devised for the courses in the programme assessed.

It would be foolish to suggest that this type of work is either straightforward or well developed as a methodology. Nevertheless, the ideas presented in this chapter should provide at least a first step for decision-makers to acquire a coherent set of information at the programme level for the purposes of strategic curriculum planning.

Chapter 5

Course development and delivery

This is the second of three chapters looking at the ways in which programme evaluation can contribute to the issues of choice, viability and quality in courses offered within the same programme. In this chapter we examine the contribution which evaluation can make in relation to the quality of courses at the design, development and presentation stages of open and distance learning courses and packages.

Evaluation design

The appearance of a course in public and its use by students is the final stage of a long process. There will have been a substantial investment of time, energy, and resources in the planning, development and preparation activities which have culminated in the course and in the decision-making which will have taken place along the way. Evaluation can be an integral part of this process from the beginning, or it can be bolted on as and when it is felt to be most appropriate.

From the evaluation perspective, it is helpful to view the process of course production and dissemination in three stages:

- Design.
- Development.
- Presentation.

The detailed evaluation plan for a course will, to a considerable extent, depend on which stage(s) you wish to focus and whether the function of the evaluation is mainly formative or summative. At this point, you will need to

---

☐ stakeholders in the evaluation
☐ role of the evaluation
☐ issues to be addressed
☐ approach to be used
☐ methodology to be used

Figure 5.1 *Framework for a course evaluation design*

clarify which questions to ask, of whom to ask them, when and in what way.

Figure 5.1 shows the key components of a course evaluation design. Once the key issues are clarified, decisions about the timing and the duration of the evaluation can then be made. An example will show how these issues link together.

Evaluation at the course design stage

The following extract is from a local open learning training materials development project for local health and welfare agencies involved with carers. Think about the evaluation design being used as you read it.

Another distinctive and essential feature of the project that was built in from its inception was that it should incorporate evaluation at every stage, in such a way that questions of success and failure would be examined throughout. The present writer had been invited to devise a strategy for evaluation as part of the original commissioning of the project, and the subsequent contract from the Kings Fund agreed that the study should 'clarify aims and methods of evaluating the implementation of the project'.

To achieve this, both in the Design Phase and in the Implementation Phase, the evaluator was given status as a full member of the Development Team, and in effect shadowed the Project coordinator – attending as an observing participant all meetings of the two Consultative Groups, all Practice Development Workshops, and the Policy Development Forums. In the Design Phase the fieldwork (carried out by this writer alone) also included accompanying the Project Coordinator on all her consultative visits and interviews and recording, monitoring and analysing the discussions of the consultation day. In the Implementation Phase, the fieldwork (carried out by the present writer with assistance . . .) also included gathering and analysing all documents that were used or devised during the Practice Development Workshops and Policy Development Forums, along with follow-up interviews with key individuals in Croydon: those who had attended Workshops or Forums or other meetings, from all levels in all of the sectors involved.

Throughout both phases, the evaluation was seen as 'formative' in that the evaluation offered feedback on a regular basis, by reporting on issues, dilemmas, perspectives and insights as they emerged during the programme. Frequently this took the form of oral reports and contributions to discussions and decision-making within the project team, and within the two consultative groups. This role was continued in the phase of package production: both the substantive findings (interview data, documentation of service policies and professional practices, conceptual frameworks, etc) and the procedures of evaluation were drawn upon in devising the learning materials (and indeed are quoted at many points in those materials as published).

Nevertheless, the evaluation was also seen, crucially, as 'summative' as well as formative. That is to say, a Final Report was envisaged which would provide an overview of progress, impact, and perceptions of success and failure in the whole project. For example, at the end of the Design Phase a summative evaluation report had been produced which identified two key 'turning points' at which significant shifts in emphasis had occurred within the project. One shift was to let questions of 'package production' take a secondary place (in the Design Phase) and to give priority to the processes of local consultation and liaison; the other was to drop the word 'training' and to emphasise the project's focus of 'development' – on bringing about real-life changes in practice, in services, and in resource allocation. (Beattie 1987)

We can use the evaluation framework described in Figure 5.1 to review the evaluation design described above.

Stakeholders in the evaluation

There are clearly a number of different stakeholders in this evaluation.

I identified:

- the evaluator himself, who had taken on an integral role as a full member of the Development Team;
- the Project coordinator and other project workers;
- the funding body (Kings Fund);
- local health and welfare agencies;
- key individuals in Croydon.

Role of the evaluation

The evaluation played both formative and summative roles, contributing both regular feedback to the project workers during the period of the project, as well as a final report to the funders at the conclusion of the project. The involvement of the evaluator from the very beginning enabled the evaluation findings to contribute to the final shape and direction of the learning package which was to be produced.

Issues to be addressed

This was a materials development project, post-project approval but pre-materials development, so the evaluation dealt with project design issues such as the aims of the package, its content, focus, and its target audience.

Approach to be used

An ethnographic or social anthropology approach was adopted by the evaluator. Ethnography is about understanding the different ways in which people view the world and how they interpret their own experiences, the better to understand the behaviour being studied. This suggests that the evaluator was in effect following the illuminative model of evaluation developed by Parlett and Hamilton (1981), using a relatively participative approach in that the potential users of the package were very much to the fore in determining and contributing to the evaluation activities.

Methodology to be used

The actual research methods described also fit the methodological strategies of the illuminative model: observation, interviews, analysis of documents and background information.

The benefits of incorporating evaluation at the design stage of the proposed learning package were threefold: it enabled the proposed course to be better fitted to the needs of its intended audiences; it increased the credibility of the proposed course among its intended audiences, and potential problem areas with respect to content and delivery were identified.

Evaluation at the course development stage

The extract above reports how the formative input during the design stage of an open and distance learning package resulted in a refocusing of the aims of the project, contributing to the change in emphasis from training to development. Evaluation can also make a key contribution during the process of drafting or developing the materials. Usually such work has to be devised as an integral part of the development process; otherwise the timetabling difficulties of incorporating changes into the design and development of the materials could be too great.

The role of the evaluation at this stage could be both formative and summative. Given the frequently high costs of development for open and distance learning materials, the pressure on those who are developing the course is usually to get it right first time. It is at this stage, however, that quality assurance procedures may operate which use the evaluation findings in a summative way in order to determine whether or not to let a course go ahead into production.

The identity of the stakeholders in the evaluation work which takes place during the course development stage will depend on the method and style of course or materials package development adopted by the course producers. At a minimum, the course designers plus those who are to support the students in their learning, the students themselves and those with overall responsibility for the programme in which the course appears will all have an investment in the development of a course which will meet the needs of all concerned.

The concern of the evaluation at this stage is usually to establish whether the course materials and course components do what the course designers intend them to do and in the way that they intend them to do it. The major areas which could present problems for either students and tutors or support staff at the presentation stage if problems were not identified and rectified at this point are:

- course component effectiveness: issues of student and tutor access, ease of use, workload;
- learning experience: the structure, clarity and degree of learner involvement in the materials and the extent and nature of the additional

support which the materials either assume or require;

- course content: relevance, accuracy, balance, topicality.

Some evaluation approaches

A number of different evaluation approaches have been developed for use during the development stage. In this next section, we will be looking at the following approaches:

- peer comment;
- instructional design input;
- student advocacy;
- quality improvement workshops;
- developmental testing;
- piloting.

Peer comment

The need for some evaluative contribution is eloquently expressed in the following extract from a paper on the problems of producing open learning materials:

> It is pointless attempting this type of writing, without being prepared to give out initial drafts for comments. Everyone accepts this. However, the reality is harder than the theory and any writer feels very vulnerable. Having inaccuracies and sections that do not work pointed out is acceptable (just about) when the overall reaction is that it is valuable material and worth doing. The real problem arises with colleagues who do not share this view, either because they are yet to be convinced that distance learning has anything to offer educationally or because they find the specific material unimpressive. (Woodcock 1990)

In this extract, Woodcock identifies three different ways in which peer comment can help an author of open learning materials:

- identifying inaccuracies;
- identifying sections which do not work;
- giving an overall reaction to the worth of the material.

The identification of inaccuracies is an absolutely essential stage in the development of materials. If they slip through at the development stage, the cost of putting them right after the materials have been produced can be considerable. The cost to the students and tutors in wasted time can only be guessed at. The identification of sections which do not work and the overall reaction to the materials from an academic or professional perspective can also be extremely useful. However there can be temptations to write for one's colleagues rather than for students. With colleagues who are inexperienced in distance and open learning, as Woodcock implies, the importance of the distinction between 'academic' writing and 'learning materials' may not be appreciated.

Instructional design input

Ross Paul, former academic vice-president of Athabasca University in Canada, has drawn attention to the need for critical input by instructional designers and editors during the development stage because of this tension between the needs of the students and the 'academic tendency' among course writers:

> . . . university academics, knowing their courses are going to be open to public scrutiny, may overload their courses, both in terms of volume and level of academic work, to ensure their academic credibility with professional peers, and it is very useful to have an instructional designer and editor there to check this tendency and to serve as student advocates in the preparation of course materials. (Paul 1990)

Paul only mentions two of the most common offences – overloading and inappropriate academic level. However there are clearly many more aspects such as assumed study skills, coherence, the friendliness of the 'voice' used, the degree to which the materials involve the student, the feedback on activities within the materials, the clarity and ease of the planning and organizational devices within the materials, the relevance to the students of the examples used and so on, which would also play a part in the learning effectiveness of the materials and which would need evaluating at the development stage.

Mary Thorpe (1993), in discussing the contribution of 'readers' to the improvement of draft materials, points out that readers need information in addition to the materials if they are to make a useful contribution to their improvement. For example they need to know who the intended learners are, the questions they will have to answer and the scale of changes to the materials which are feasible within the time and resources available.

Student advocacy

One (very common) solution to the problem of representing the student perspective during the development of materials is to recruit people to use or to comment on the materials 'as if' they were students. Their comments and reactions can be collected relatively informally and, because they focus on the detail within the materials, can be very helpful. But of course, these commentators will usually be focusing only on one part of what will eventually become a coordinated and complex package.

Quality improvement workshops

These are described by Mouli and Ramakrishna as follows:

> In a series of such workshop sessions the APOU [Andhra Pradesh Open University] gathered information regarding the course materials from its counsellors and learners. The 'quality improvement workshops' had representatives from among course writers, subject experts, tutor-counsellors and students. Attempts were made to estimate student expectations and needs and to see how far they were met through the materials. (Mouli and Ramakrishna 1991)

Developmental testing

Even with constructive and informed input from expert colleagues, instructional designers and 'student advocates', problems can still arise with materials. Two other types of approach are available to course developers which can produce useful inputs: developmental testing and piloting.

To a certain extent the two techniques overlap. Developmental testing involves the process of testing the study materials as an intrinsic part of their development. Ideally, the aim is to get students to work through the materials while they are in draft form in order to identify problems with aspects such as clarity of aims and objectives, sequencing, logic, retention of interest, comprehension, difficulty level, workload, feasibility of student activities, and so on. There are major problems with the organization of developmental testing however. Some you may have already experienced yourself.

The major problem is one of trying to replicate the conditions in which the students of the course will be carrying out their studies. This means that test students should be found who are willing to work right through the course and that they should use all the components which the actual students will be expected to use. The reality is that few people are willing to put in the effort or have the commitment to study seriously and in depth over any sort of extended period without some form of extrinsic reward. Thus developmental testers, even when paid, can have rather a high drop-out rate (Nathenson and Henderson 1976, Zand 1993). There is also the problem that all the components including student support are unlikely to be ready and available to use for testing at the same time. A number of different solutions have therefore been devised in attempts to deal with such problems.

One attempted solution to the very high drop-out which can occur with developmental testers is to persuade the institution to allow the award of a credit for the successful completion of the draft course. The chief problem here is that of timing. If the course is sufficiently well developed for developmental testers to be awarded credit, then usually the institution would prefer to be able to offer it publicly. In fact a number of models have been devised which work on the basis of detailed developmental testing of the course as a whole during its early presentations.

Rolling remake Detailed comments and feedback about the course components, the manner of their presentation, the teaching process and their content are collected for different stages of the course. Over, say, a five-year period, each stage will be developmentally tested and that part remade on the basis of the feedback which has been received. Thus at the end of five years, the course will have been fully tested and fully remade.

'1+4', '1+5', '1+6' These are models which operate on the basis of a single year's initial presentation (or in some cases a two-year presentation) during which intensive, detailed and sustained feedback is gathered from students. After this, the course is remade on the basis of all the feedback. The costs are covered by making the course last much longer than usual after the initial remake, hence the '1+5' title. This means that the course lasts for one year, is remade, then is presented for a further five years before it is again remade to update it.

Piloting

In effect, rolling remakes and the $x+y$ model are forms of piloting. Probably the main difference between piloting and developmental testing is that with developmental testing the people responsible for the development of the material also carry the responsibility for testing, whereas the piloting of materials or courses tends to be undertaken by those who organize and actually run the course. However as Barbara Flagg (1990) points out in relation to the the formative evaluation of television programmes:

> Evaluators communicate the formative findings and action recommendations to the designers, producers, and programmers who weigh them along with data on time, money, personnel and so on, when making revision decisions for the final programme. Note, however, that formative evaluation is of little use at this point if the pilot versions cannot be modified. Under those circumstances, the findings

inform the development of other programmes of the same or similar projects.

The use of an initial package to test out or pilot an approach in order to inform the development or selection and use of other courses is frequently used in training settings. The following example describes how a standard off-the-shelf training package was used as the basis of a ten-day in-house management training programme.

> Evaluating the effectiveness of particular training programmes has always been difficult, ranging from the use of financial measures (such as increased sales, reduced costs) to subjective measures of change seen in behaviour of participants after training. In this instance several measures were used.

> Financial . . .
> Participants information [on content, format, material provided and benefit to themselves] . . .
> Observation . . .
> Follow-up . . .

> Having now used package material to provide the first management training programme at Viking Packing Group, and identified several areas for consideration, I shall now be able to offer another programme which is more relevant and appropriate to the industrial setting in which the participants work. (Jeynes 1990)

No single approach described above is ideal. The particular approach adopted by any particular team of course designers must depend on the circumstances, the constraints and the context within which they are working.

Evaluation at the course presentation stage

With conventional face-to-face provision, the tutor will receive a range of informal feedback from students about the relevance and quality of the course. The attendance of the students at lectures or tutorials, the enthusiasm and knowledge they display in their oral, practical and written work, their comments to the tutor and their success in assessment will all combine to give the tutor a great deal of information about the learning effectiveness of the course. However, with open and distance learning, there may be little or no direct contact between the course designers, the course providers and the students. Course feedback may be the main if not the only channel of communication between the students and those who carry the responsibility for their teaching. In effect, course evaluation at the presentation stage has to act as the students' voice. At the same time, there may also be support and tutorial staff working with the students who will have their own views on the learning effectiveness of the course and on the role they are expected to undertake.

Stakeholders

Different groups will have a vested interest in the quality of the course at the point of presentation. Students, tutors, course designers, programme managers, funding agencies and the employers and other future beneficiaries of the skills and knowledge acquired from the course by the student will all have an interest in one or more of the three basic questions.

- Does the course achieve its aims?
- Has the students' experience of the course been a satisfactory one?
- Is the course viable?

If the programme managers are to establish whether or not they are meeting the needs of the different stakeholders, they will need to treat each of these groups both as potential sources of information as well as recipients of information. For example, where an employer is the sponsor of either the student or the course, then it is important to get feedback on their perception of the quality and value of the course. Figure 5.2 (overleaf) shows an example of a page from a questionnaire to employers who have sponsored students on open learning management education courses.

As you can see from question 12, the courses are offered in Hungary. They are part of the UK government's assistance to Hungary to deal with its transition to a market economy. The question therefore asks not only about the relevance of the courses for the employees as individuals, and the employer's organization, but also about the employer's perception of its relevance to national needs (Farnes, Woodley and Ashby 1993).

Approaches

Evaluation at the course presentation stage does not consist only of course evaluation. In order to answer the questions raised by the stakeholders, information on issues related to student progress and outcomes of study will also need to form part of the evaluation activities. The achievement of the aims of the course and the extent to which students have a satisfactory learning experience will be affected by a mix of course related factors,

11. How much does the student appear to **use what has been learnt** from the course(s) in his or her work with the following people? *(Ring one on each row)*

Uses ideas from the course(s) with	Very much	Quite a lot	To some extent	Not at all	Don't know	
You, as the student's boss 1	2	3	4	5	*(40)*
Student's colleagues in similar grades.....1	2	3	4	5	*(41)*
Student's subordinates...........................1	2	3	4	5	*(42)*
Student's clients/customers..................1	2	3	4	5	*(43)*

12. In terms of Hungary's transition to a market economy how **relevant** do you think the courses are for your employees, your organisation, and Hungary - now and in the future? *(Ring one number in each column)*

Relevance of the courses for :	Your employees Now In future		Your organisation Now In future		Hungary Now In future	
Very relevant................1 *(44)*	1 *(45)*		1 *(46)*	1 *(47)*	1 *(48)*	1 *(49)*
Quite relevant...............2	2		2	2	2	2
Somewhat relevant.......3	3		3	3	3	3
Not very relevant...........4	4		4	4	4	4
Not at all relevant..........5	5		5	5	5	5

13. Do you consider these courses to be **value for money**? *(Ring one only)*

Very good value for money.............1   *(50)*
Quite good value for money 2
Reasonable value for money 3
Not very good value for money 4
Very poor value for money.............5
Don't know 6

14. As you know these courses are taught 'at a distance' using printed booklets, video, audio and computer software and occasional tutorials. What is your view of the **benefits** of this method of teaching for your organisation? Select the **three** most important benefits from the following statements. *(Ring three of the statements below)*

Students can study in their own time and at their own pace.....................................1   *(51)*
Students do not have to take time away from their work 2   *(52)*
Multi-media teaching allows for different learning styles 3   *(53)*
Distance teaching involves part time study spread over a long period 4   *(54)*
Students can apply what they learn to their work as they study.............................5   *(55)*
Learning on your own can be more efficient than learning in a group 6   *(56)*
Distance teaching is more flexible than traditional teaching 7   *(57)*
Students need more self-discipline to study...8   *(58)*
The costs of distance teaching to the employer are lower 9   *(59)*
Other *(please write in)* 1   *(60)*

....

....

(61-64)

Figure 5.2 *Extract from questionnaire to students' employers*
Source: Farnes, Woodley & Ashby, 1993

Course components: their usefulness, helpfulness, relative
importance, ease of use, workload, difficulty level

Learning experience: difficulties experienced, growth of confidence,
development of study skills, quality of interaction
with materials, use of support

Course content: relevance, interest, challenge, use of existing
knowledge

Students' personal study environment: access to media, access to
components, extent, duration and periodicity of
study time available, study pattern

Student outcomes: achievement of personal and course aims,
understanding, competences, outputs achieved

Figure 5.3 *Main categories of student feedback topics*

personal factors, and institutional factors. The viability of the course will depend to a considerable extent on the answers to these questions.

Student feedback

Student feedback can provide information on a range of key issues at the course presentation stage. Figure 5.3 lists some of the main categories.

Figure 5.4 shows two contrasting examples of the concerns about course components on which student feedback can shed light. In Figure 5.4a the question focuses on the degree of use of all the different components, including media and the alternative forms of support available to students in different regions.

In Figure 5.4b the questions concentrate on just one of the components, albeit the main teaching component. The questions focus on the detail of the way in which students used different facilities of an interactive video, and on any changes in their level of confidence at different points. In other words, these questions are investigating the students' experience of using this component rather than just the the level of use as in the question in Figure 5.4a.

Figure 5.5 shows an extract from a questionnaire template used by the University of South Australia for courses offered by its distance teaching unit (Nunan 1992). This particular extract shows the questions relating to the subject content. One of the aims of the course evaluation here is to help with staff development. The intention is that by encouraging and helping

2 Students use different amounts of the components of Open University courses.
   How much did **you use** each of the SD206 components listed below?
   On the 5-point scale below, the top category, 'Fully', means that you used a component as much as was reasonably possible in this particular course; for example, reading all or nearly all of the Six Books, or listening to all of the audiocassette material.

SD206 components	Not at all				Fully	Not available in my region	
The Six Books 1	2	3	4	5			*(19) (20-23)*
Introduction and Guide 1	2	3	4	5			*(24)*
TV and Radio Notes (in Broadcast (and Video) Notes) . .1	2	3	. 4	5			*(25)*
AV Notes 1	2	3	4	5			*(26)*
Video Notes (in Broadcast (and Video) Notes) 1	2	3	4	5			*(27)* *(28)*
Other printed materials (e.g. Guide to Designing Experiments in the Behavioural Sciences) 1	2	3	4	5			*(29)*
Television broadcasts 1	2	3	4	5			*(30)*
OU videorecordings of TV broadcasts (loan scheme). . . 1	2	3	4	5			*(31)*
Videocassettes (non-broadcast) 1	2	3	4	5			*(32)*
Radio broadcasts 1	2	3	4	5			*(33)*
Audiocassettes 1	2	3	4	5			*(34)*
Home Kit 1	2	3	4	5			*(35)*
Computer-based activities at Summer School 1	2	3	4	5			*(36)*
TMAs as consolidation of learning (incl. Project) 1	2	3	4	5			*(37)*
Tutor comments on TMAs 1	2	3	4	5			*(38)* *(39)*
CMAs as consolidation of learning 1	2	3	4	5			*(40)*

Ring 0 for any service not available in your region. Answer as normal for those that were available.

	Not at all				Fully	Not available	
Tutorials at study centre 1	2	3	4	5		0	*(41)*
Group telephone tutorials 1	2	3	4	5		0	*(42)*
Individual phone contact with tutor for advice 1	2	3	4	5		0	*(43)*
Counselling 1	2	3	4	5		0	*(44)*
Self-help study groups 1	2	3	4	5		0	*(45)*
Half-day school(s) 1	2	3	4	5		0	*(46)*
Day school(s) 1	2	3	4	5		0	*(47)*
Summer School 1	2	3	4	5			*(48)*

Figure 5.4a. *Example of question on degree of use of different course components*
Source: Field 1993

6. Did you experience any problems in operating the
    IV workstation while using the training material?   Yes   1   *(24)*
                                                          No   2

    If Yes, did you do any of the following to get help
    (Ring all that apply)
        refer to the HELP option of the Main Menu?   1   *(25)*
        refer to the User Guide for the package?   1   *(26)*
        ask one of the Training Department staff for
        assistance?   1   *(27)*
        ask another IV user for assistance?   1   *(28)*
        something else *(Please specify:........................)*   1   *(29)*

7. How confident did you feel about using the 'mouse' to
    control the IV:

	Very confident			Not at all confident		
– before starting on Part 1?	1	2	3	4	5	*(30)*
– after completing Part 1?	1	2	3	4	5	*(31)*

Figure 5.4b. *Example of questions on the process of using a specific course component*
Source: Kirkwood 1992

staff to carry out evaluations of the courses on which they teach, those staff who have less experience of the rather special demands of open and distance teaching will benefit from the insights provided from student feedback.

These three examples illustrate the question of who carries out the student feedback and how it is related to the purpose of the evaluation. For instance the first example (Figure 5.4a) comes from a regular study carried out internally at the UK Open University. It gathers the same data from students on different courses and in different programmes of study. This enables comparisons to be made between different courses at any one time, and between different years to monitor any changes over time. The data is effective as an initial mesh for identifying problem areas, but further detailed research would need to be carried out to investigate the causes of any problems thus identified.

The second example (Figure 5.4b) comes from a 'one-off' evaluation which we have already briefly discussed, carried out by a joint external and internal team. The study was designed to examine the learning effectiveness, user–machine interaction, organizational impact and cost effectiveness of a new type of interactive-video-based course at British Telecom. The design included feedback from trainers as well as trainees,

The teaching process

1 I had no difficulties in   SA   A   N   D   SD   NA
   contacting my lecturer ...
   Additional comment

2 The teaching approach within   SA   A   N   D   SD   NA
   the Study guide encouraged
   me to interact with the
   materials of the subject and
   the lecturer ...
   Additional comment

3 The workload in studying the   SA   A   N   D   SD   NA
   subject and completing the
   assignment requirements was
   reasonable ...
   Additional comment

Key to the characters
SA   – Strongly agree
A   – Agree
N   – Neutral
D   – Disagree
SD   – Strongly disagree

Figure 5.5 *Template questions for feedback on the teaching process*
Source: Nunan 1992, p 5

and from line managers and others with a stake in the skills and competences acquired by the trainees, and also used a variety of different approaches, both quantitative and qualitative.

The third example (Figure 5.5) comes from a regular series of studies which are carried out internally by teaching staff at the University of Western Australia. Staff are encouraged to get student feedback as a form of staff development. The feedback is seen as a way of helping those staff who lack experience in distance learning to reflect critically on their teaching in respect to the special needs of students who study at a distance. The advantage of this approach is that teachers get formative feedback on their courses, while at the same time it is quite clear who has control over the evaluation and what the purpose of the evaluation is. The disadvantage of this approach is that the feedback does not contribute to any central monitoring of either the courses or the operation and effectiveness of the support system.

10. If I were asked to summarise the three most important factors or group of factors in my decision to withdraw, these would be:

Please circle three numbers

1 Course of study
2 Academic preparedness
3 Teaching/learning situation and institutional atmosphere
4 Course commitment/motivation to study
5 Accommodation/distance/travel problems
6 Finance/job
7 Family relationship/family problems
8 Health/accident/stress
9 Other personal factors

11. If you indicated that anything under items 1, 2 or 3 were the most important influence, please give us some more details so we can try to improve things.

Figure 5.6 *Extract from questionnaire to students who withdrew from a course*
Source: Abbott-Chapman et al 1992, p 142

Finally we look at an example of student feedback which is not course specific. Figure 5.6 is an extract from a questionnaire to students on a conventional face-to-face course who had withdrawn from their studies, and who had indicated earlier in the questionnaire that the course itself had played a major role in their decision to withdraw.

For information which focuses on the difficulties which students experience with their courses, both successful and unsuccessful students need to be involved in the evaluation.

Methodology and timing

Methods for collecting data

It is perhaps inevitable that in open and distance learning, the major form of data collection should be by means of self-completion questionnaires. The questionnaires used in the examples shown all use either pre-coded answers or a mixture of pre-coded questions and open questions where the student or other respondent can write their answer in their own words. However, you are not limited to self-completion questionnaires by any means. Less structured approaches such as group discussions may be more appropriate for identifying issues of concern and increasing understanding of processes from the perspective of the participants. Diary feedback can give details about the process of study, and the ways in which problems were tackled. Employers and other institutional stakeholders may be more easily reached through telephone interviews, or through personal contact. The fact remains, however, that for formal systematic feedback, structured self-completion questionnaires are usually the most appropriate tool for collecting quantitative data.

Research design

The quality of the data collected through questionnaires can vary considerably. The relevance, flexibility and sensitivity of the questions, and the level of response which can be expected using self-completion questionnaires can all give grounds for concern. As with any research, the quality of the data collected will reflect the care taken with the development, preparation and organization of the fieldwork.

Questionnaires are like any other course materials in that they need a considerable amount of thought and care in their construction and design if the potential respondents are to find them interesting and easy to complete. A well-structured questionnaire which is logically sequenced, with clear instructions, well laid out, and which asks the respondent about issues in which they are interested will get high-quality responses from a good percentage of the sample; particularly if a personal letter explaining the purpose of the study accompanies the questionnaire. For example, the annual study from which the question in Figure 5.4a is taken regularly achieves a response rate of between 70 and 90 per cent.

However, there is undoubtedly a tension between the ease of analysis which pre-coded answers offer and the greater opportunity for students to offer more detailed and specific comment offered by open questions which is offset by a considerable analysis commitment if the answers are to be content-analysed for quantification. It should be said, however, that if students feel strongly about their experience with a course, the invitation to complete a feedback form does not necessarily inhibit them from sending in more detailed comment. The closely typed six-page critique of one course received from a disappointed student by a course designer of my acquaintance is perhaps unusual, but nevertheless substantial additional comments from students are by no means uncommon.

Timing, frequency and duration

The level of detail which can be collected through questionnaire-type feedback does depend to a considerable extent on the timing and duration of the feedback requests to students. The examples shown earlier were all from questionnaires which were designed to get feedback from students at the end of the course. This approach does limit the level of detail which can be investigated in that accurate recall of the detail of difficulties experienced does fade very quickly. While this may not be a problem with short two-or three-day courses, it can present considerable problems for longer courses. One way of dealing with this is to collect feedback from students during the presentation of the course. This can be on a regular basis, unit by unit, or on a periodic basis, say at three points during the course. The exact timing would depend very much on the length of the course.

At the same time, the frequency with which students can realistically be approached to give detailed feedback is severely limited. Too many requests would lead to both the response rate and the quality of the information dropping sharply. It would also be unfair in the demands on the time of the individual. At the UK Open University, we have tried to limit the number of approaches to individual students for evaluation purposes to no more that two per year.

Finally there is the question of the frequency with which student feedback is sought for any one course. This decision will be constrained by the resources available and the purpose of the evaluation. If the aim is to provide feedback to the tutors for staff development purposes, or to provide a quality assurance mechanism which gives students the opportunity to feed their views about the course back to the programme managers, then there is a strong argument for carrying out feedback on a regular basis. If the numbers are small and the data collection and analysis is routinized, then feedback might take place during or after every presentation. On the other hand, if numbers of students are large and if the purpose of the feedback is primarily formative, then a feedback study which involves only a sample of students on those occasions when there have been changes to the course materials would be appropriate.

Conclusion

The potential of evaluation to monitor and to improve the quality of courses at the design, development and presentation stages is quite clear. However the students' learning experience is much more than just their interaction with the course components. The individual student has to learn the rules of the organization providing the course and must learn to operate successfully within the regulatory and organizational constraints of the institution which is offering the course. In the next chapter, we will be examining how evaluation can help you get a view of the student's experience as a whole, in order to identify ways in which the organization of the programme may be made more 'student friendly'.

Chapter 6

Student recruitment and support services

In this chapter we look at the structures and support systems insofar as they relate to the teaching process and the provision of open and distance learning courses. The aim is to examine how evaluation can help you view programme provision as a whole from the perspective of the student in order to get a better understanding of how evaluation can contribute to the more effective functioning of the student service areas.

Pre-registration issues

The focus of all the concern and activity, the people who are to benefit from the carefully designed and constructed courses, are the students. They are on the receiving end of a whole range of different aspects of the course presentation system. Figure 6.1 represents the interaction of the different service systems with the teaching system.

The point is that even if the pedagogic aspects of a course are all tested and well structured, the experience of entry into and participation in the programme may be spoiled for the student if any aspects of the service systems are not operating as they should be; for example, if enquirers get their materials late, or if information about courses or workshops is inaccurate. If you are trying to design a system of evaluation which will take into account the overall experience of the student within the institution, you will need to consider including some form of evaluation of the student interface with these associated service systems.

The flow diagram in Figure 6.2 shows each successive stage in the recruitment process from awareness that the learning or training

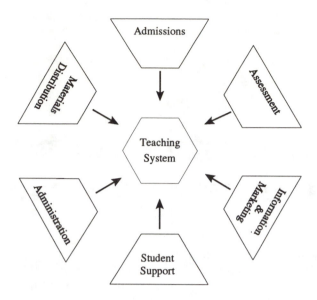

Figure 6.1 *Interaction of service systems with the teaching system*

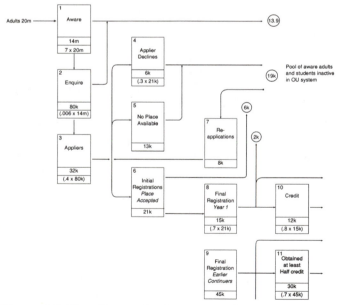

Figure 6.2 *Flow diagram showing stages in the recruitment process*
Source: Field 1982, p 129

opportunity exists to actually applying for a place. In the figure, six different groups of students or clients who are potential students are identified. In the following sections, we will be considering the extent to which the interests of these groups need to be represented through the programme evaluation process.

Information and marketing

If you have designed or developed a course or a programme of courses with particular target groups in mind, perhaps after having carried out careful needs assessment and market research, you will want to ensure that the right people are aware that your courses are available. Think about your own organization, and the information and marketing strategies it uses for open and distance learning courses. What aspects do you feel should be included in evaluating its effectiveness? Some ideas about the sorts of issues you might be interested in are listed below.

- Do the people you are trying to attract on to your programmes of study know of your existence?
- Is people's knowledge about the organization and its programmes of courses accurate?
- Is the right information getting to the right people?
- Are enquiries being handled satisfactorily from the users' point of view?
- How easy is it to get hold of an application form for your programme of study?

In the following sections we will be looking in more detail at these issues with the aim of identifying just what aspects may be useful for you to build in as part of your programme evaluation.

Awareness of programme provision

Clearly the size of the pool of applicants on which a course or a programme draws will depend to a large extent on the proportion of the target group who are aware that the courses are available. The distribution of public awareness in terms of geography, location within a company and socio-economic status, can tell you much about the success of the marketing and information effort. For example, for many years now the Open University has regularly monitored the UK general population about its awareness of the OU as an institution, and about its courses and the special features of the University. Figure 6.3 shows how public awareness has increased from 31 per cent in 1971 to 87 per cent in 1993. In this way, senior management have been able to monitor changes over time in awareness among certain

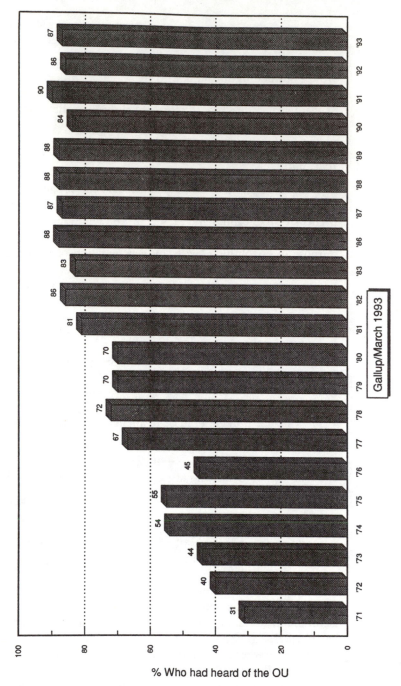

Figure 6.3 *Public awareness of OU provision*
Source: Social Surveys (Gallup Poll) Ltd 1993

key groups. They are also able to monitor the accuracy of the information which was getting through.

Thinking about your own organization, who would be the most appropriate groups to monitor in terms of their awareness of your provision? Your answers will depend very much on whether you are providing for a closed population, such as certain categories of staff in a particular company, or people who live in a certain geographical area, or, perhaps, people in a particular profession. Whatever your answers, you need to know whether your target groups, and indeed your potential clients, are aware of the programmes you offer and of the benefits to them of those particular programmes.

How do you make contact with members of your target group for the purpose of establishing the level of penetration of your message? For this type of information, it is essential that the data is statistically valid, that it comes from a representative sample or a full census if you are only dealing with a small population. It does not matter what method you use to contact people for this type of study – face-to-face, phone, postal survey – but a sound sample design and a good response rate are essential if you are going to make estimates from the data.

Enquirers

The enquiry phase plays a key role in linking potential students to the institution. Frequently some details are kept about enquiries. Think about your own institution. Are you familiar with the procedures for dealing with enquiries? Is any record of each enquiry kept?

- Address of inquirer – an analysis will give an indication of the geographical spread of enquirers.
- Details of query – an analysis will give details about the sorts of topics people have an interest in studying; the sorts of questions they would like information on.
- Where did you hear about us? – a commonly used but extremely useful way of getting feedback on contact sources for different groups in different areas.

It must be said, however, that there can be a great danger of too much data being collected at this stage with no procedures being set up to gather together this information and analyze it. This data can be very useful as feedback on what messages are getting through to whom, and on what is not getting through that people want to know about, but only if the data is actually analyzed and fed through to the person or people who can make use of it.

Non-applicants

Non-applicants are people who have enquired about a course or a programme but who have not followed through their initial interest with an application for a place. Can you think of why it may be important for you to find out why this is?

- The person's personal circumstances may make it inconvenient at the moment.
- The way the enquiry was handled may have deterred the person from pursuing the idea of an application.
- The course/programme the person wanted is not available at all/at the time it was wanted/in the form it was wanted/at the price that was wanted.

The three groups of reasons listed above each suggest possible areas for further research and evaluation. The reason it may be worth considering looking further at this group is that you know that they are already interested in study or training, and that they were interested enough to take the trouble to make an enquiry. If there are problems with the way enquiries are being handled, then you need to know about the problem quickly so that it can be rectified. If the problem falls into one of the other two categories, then you still need to know about it in case changes in provision or in the regulations are possible. The use of information and the adoption of ideas from this group may well help to minimize the loss of people at this stage.

Recruitment and selection

Guidance

Part of the application process may well include some guidance for applicants. Advice can vary from the provision of a detailed personal session with someone, either face-to-face or on the phone, the provision of detailed and often complex information booklets, or simply including very brief instructions with the application form. Whatever form the guidance available to your students takes, you will need to know:

- whether the applicants are aware that it is available;
- whether those who might benefit from the advice actually use it;
- if they do use it, whether it is useful;
- how accurate the information is which is given to them.

Applications

It can be crucial to monitor carefully the people who make an application to join your course or programme. Unless you are always able to accept everyone who wishes to join a course whenever they apply, then the data about your applicants may also have to serve as a basis of selection, and as a means of ensuring that there is no bias or discrimination in your selection procedures.

Selection

The question of selection of students is an important one. If the selection is being carried out by intermediaries, for example if departmental heads select those of their staff whom they wish to take a specific course, then the criteria they are applying will need to be clear, explicit and open to monitoring. Selection may just mean imposing some sort of queuing procedure, or it may mean choosing a sub-group of those who have applied on the basis of the possession of some attribute. Consider the following example: a course for middle-managers is only open to those who have completed three years in a management position. If you were to carry out an evaluation of the selection system, what aspects would you want to see included? The sorts of issues I would consider including are:

- Establish the aims of the selection criteria – what outcome are they trying to achieve?
- Are the selection criteria actually being applied as set out in the regulations?
- What are the outcomes – are they the ones being aimed for?
- What are the other effects of having these selection criteria – on different groups of stakeholders, on the courses and programmes?

Non-acceptors

Even after applicants have received the offer of a place, they may choose not to accept the offer. Whatever the size of your organization, the existence of this group can make planning difficult. It can also mean lost revenue, and it may be an indicator that there is a problem in the system which needs attention. Typical of the sorts of reasons a person might have for not taking up the offer of a place are:

- their personal circumstances have now changed;
- they forgot to respond to the offer and missed the deadline;
- they decided to go somewhere else.

The reasons which people who do not take up the offer of a place give when asked about their decision can tell you a lot about the effects of competition and who the competition is, whether people are having problems in fitting in with your regulations, whether they are too complex or the application period too extended, and whether additional guidance or counselling may be needed for applicants so that problems can be anticipated, or possible options identified for the individual. For example, if there is some sort of financial problem, there may be a financial assistance fund or special scheme about which they could be given information.

The major problems in carrying out any evaluation of this group are in fact likely to be ones of making contact and of getting the people involved to participate in your evaluation research. The less involved a person feels with an organization, the less likely they are to want to participate in any research activities which are primarily for its benefit. This does not mean that research is impossible with this group; but it does mean that considerable care will have to be taken in following them up. Personal interviews either by telephone or face-to-face, although expensive, are likely to yield much better response rates than postal questionnaires or invitations to participate in group discussions.

Teaching and support systems

Student support issues

As Mary Thorpe pointed out when discussing the problems of evaluating counselling provision, a wide variety of approaches for supporting students are used by different organizations (Thorpe 1993). Some provide continuing support from the first point of contact before the student has even applied for the course. This may be the case particularly where certain groups have been targeted for recruitment. Others may have a brief induction for new students, and then leave them to get on with their studies, responding to any requests for help or information as and when they occur. This help and information may be provided by a variety of people in different departments of the organization.

Organizational policy may be to encourage such variation within a particular programme, with different approaches being used in different locations. Where this is the case, then local evaluation studies may need to be considered. There are several ways in which this can be organized:

- organized and carried out locally;
- organized centrally and carried out locally;
- organized and carried out centrally.

Clearly there are advantages and disadvantages to each of these strategies. The major advantage of evaluation which is carried out locally is that it can be tailored to meet particular local circumstances and needs. However, there will be a danger of lack of comparability of the information if it is collected in different ways in different areas. This problem will be compounded where the studies are also designed locally. One way to minimize this problem is to provide centrally designed guidelines for the collection of data, or templates for questionnaires to students.

However, there is a range of issues where information is needed by the programme decision-makers centrally. These include:

- Identifying what is actually happening in terms of induction, preparation and support of students.
- Establishing whether students have
  - sufficient knowledge of availability of preparation and support services;
  - ease of access to services; and
  - realistic expectations of what might be provided.
- Other issues which need to be established are which students actually use the service, what do they get, and does the service offered meet students' needs with respect to content, structure, timing, accessibility?

Although course-based studies can and should cover such issues, the information gathered only indicates how well or badly such services are operating for that particular course. For feedback on how a service is operating overall, some form of student-based study will be needed. If information about both the services overall and in specific courses is required, then the sample design will need to reflect the dual purpose of the study, with due weighting being given for students who may be registered for more than one course.

Functioning of the teaching related systems

The major systems will vary between different open and distance learning organizations, but the principle is common; namely, that the students' experience of study will be determined both by the pedagogic quality of the courses for which they are enroled and by the efficiency and effectiveness of the teaching related systems. Not all courses will necessarily use all the teaching related systems. For example courses which consist only of study packages may have no tuition and no assessment, or personal development courses may not use the assessment system.

The major questions relating to the information and non-academic support systems have already been discussed, but issues relating to the other systems could include such aspects as:

- whether course components are delivered in time for scheduled study;
- whether the turn-round time for marking is adhered to; whether the quality of feedback on assignments is adequate; whether the marking is seen to be fair, and whether the appeal system is understood and seen as satisfactory;
- whether the availability and responsiveness of tuition staff is satisfactory.

The range of options which are available for evaluating such a range of issues are as wide as for other areas of activity (see Figure 6.4). Essentially there are four types of option:

- passive/student initiated feedback received on an ad hoc basis;
- passive/student initiated feedback organized on a systematic basis;
- active feedback on an ad hoc basis;
- active feedback sought on a systematic basis.

Passive feedback received on an ad hoc basis is simply what might be described as the shriek method, whereby things are assumed to be operating as intended unless someone shrieks. The institution may claim to be alert to any concerns expressed by students, but does nothing to seek out information about concerns in any active or systematic way.

Passive feedback which is organized on a systematic basis is quite a common feedback method. Here, the student is provided with the means to comment or raise matters of concern, but no further action is taken by the institution to encourage student response or seek out student opinion. Feedback cards inserted into materials are a common means of data collection using this method.

	Passive	Active
Ad Hoc	✓	✓
Systematic	✓	✓

Figure 6.4 *Feedback options for monitoring teaching related systems*

Active feedback organized on an ad hoc basis usually consists of some form of special study which addresses specific concerns. These may have been identified as requiring further investigation either through passive feedback or from systematic feedback.

Active feedback organized on a systematic basis usually provides a monitoring function. Regular feedback will provide measures of any changes over time as well as data on current levels of satisfaction and areas of concern.

These options are not mutually exclusive and may indeed all be used in varying degrees within the same evaluation programme. The examples which follow are approaches which all operate in the same organization.

Monitoring the quality of teaching related services

Different types of evaluation approaches can be appropriate for this aspect of provision for students. I would like to describe three rather different approaches recently tried out at the Open University as part of its work in trying to improve its monitoring of the quality of services to students:

- A student initiated response system.
- A special student postal survey.
- Staff and student workshops.

Example of system using student initiated response

The first example is the 'Quality Issue Card System' (QIC). An example of the feedback card provided by the programme organizers for students is shown in Figure 6.5. This particular system was set up by the Open Business School with three aims (Cameron and Holloway 1992):

- to provide students with a simple route for feeding in reports of problems and other comments, reducing the risk that they will write to 'The Open University, Milton Keynes' and get lost in the system and increasing the chance that they will receive a prompt and helpful reply;
- to help us to build up a clearer picture of common types of problems, so we can concentrate resources on preventing them happening in the future;
- to assist MECs [Management Education Coordinators] and course teams in compiling their own logs of problem areas or comments for attention.

All MBA students received a sheet of cards with their first mailing. This was accompanied by a letter of welcome from the MBA Director in which she

MBA QUALITY ISSUE CARD

FOR OFFICE USE
R ☐☐/☐☐☐

Please return this card to the Management Education Co-ordinator at your Regional Centre.
I should like to express satisfaction/dissatisfaction with the following issue(s):

_____

_____

_____

_____

Course to which the above relates _____

Name: _____   Tele. No. (if convenient to be telephoned)

Personal Identifier _____   Day: _____

Eve: _____

Figure 6.5 *Extract from MBA 'QIC' card*
Source: Open University

'set out some quality standards which the MBA programme was aiming for, and indicated who to contact in the first instance in the event of any problems'. This system was itself the source of regular review to ensure that any problems in the way it was operating were ironed out. From this it emerged that relatively few students actually use it. (Approximately 6 per cent in the first six months (Swift 1992).) It was also found that cards were sent 'about a wide range of issues ranging from pointing out a typo to challenging the whole exam system. There are also some congratulatory comments, and some constructive observations' (Cameron and Holloway 1992).

The quality group who introduced the scheme concluded that in resource terms, it took up less time than dealing with queries in an ad hoc manner, and were planning to carry on with the scheme, refining and modifying it as and when it seemed necessary.

Special student postal survey
The second example was a student postal survey which was sent out to samples of MBA students some six months after the the QIC card system had been in operation. The four-page questionnaire used a mixture of

closed and open questions, asking students to rate aspects of the support they had received using a five-point scale. An extract from this questionnaire is shown in Figure 6.6.

The survey was sent out anonymously, so the usual procedure of sending out reminders to students could not be followed. Nevertheless, the researcher was able to report a response rate of 50 per cent. She commented that 'The quality of the replies was good and there were substantial and thoughtful comments in answers to the open-ended questions. Where there is specific comment on the Audit initiative, it is to welcome it' (Swift 1992). Both quantitative and qualitative data were analysed, with the open-ended

1. How do you rate B881 in terms of various items listed below?

> Please ring one code for each item in the range 1 = poor to 5 =excellent. *See also additional instructions below in relation to use of codes 6 and 7.*

	Poor				*Excellent*	*Did not use*	*Not applicable*	
The whole course in terms of meeting your learning objectives	1	2	3	4	5			(9)
The user-friendliness of the course materials	1	2	3	4	5			(10)
Delivery of materials in time for scheduled study	1	2	3	4	5			(11)
Course team's assessment of the time needed for study	1	2	3	4	5			(12)
The value for money of the course	1	2	3	4	5			(13)

The course materials
Note: Ring 6 if your did not use the materials/services, etc. provided: ring 7 if not applicable for your course/in your case

						Did not use	*Not applicable*	
Course units	1	2	3	4	5	6		(14)
Reader(s)	1	2	3	4	5	6	7	(15)
Set book(s)	1	2	3	4	5	6	7	(16)
Supplementary readings	1	2	3	4	5	6	7	(17)
Videocassette(s)	1	2	3	4	5	6	7	(18)
Audiocassette(s)	1	2	3	4	5	6	7	(19)
The computer software	1	2	3	4	5	6	7	(20)
PC-based teaching/learning	1	2	3	4	5	6	7	(21)
CoSy conferencing, as complementing the teaching	1	2	3	4	5	6	7	(22)
In-text activities, as devices to help your learning/ understanding of the material in the course units	1	2	3	4	5	6		(23)
The TMAs as consolidation of your learning	1	2	3	4	5	6		(24)

Tutor and support for learning

Teaching comments on your scripts and the PT3s	1	2	3	4	5	6		(25)
Fairness of the grading of your TMAs	1	2	3	4	5	6		(26)
Speed of return of your TMAs	1	2	3	4	5	6		(27)
Face-to-face tutorials/day schools	1	2	3	4	5	6		(28)
Tutor accessibility, if you had queries	1	2	3	4	5	6	7	(29)
Tutor/counsellor support if you had problems	1	2	3	4	5	6	7	(30)
Benefit from membership of a 'self help' group	1	2	3	4	5	6	7	(31)

Figure 6.6 *Extract from MBA Audit Questionnaire*
Source: Swift 1992

comments all being typed up for reference. The advantages of the survey approach are that

- managers are given an accurate picture of students' opinions about a range of services at a particular moment in time;
- aspects which are working well can be monitored as well as those where there are problems;
- it is possible to identify the relative success of different areas in providing a satisfactory service for students.

It should be noted that the issues were those chosen by the provider as being important and therefore they reflect the provider's perspective.

Staff and student workshops

In the third example, a series of three workshops were held in different parts of the country. The aim of these workshops was to identify those issues relating to the quality of the service which was offered to students and part-time staff which students and staff themselves felt should be monitored on a regular basis. In each of three Regional Centres, approximately a dozen students and four or five part-time staff were brought together for a workshop scheduled to last for three hours. Structured group discussion methods were used to promote full and frank exchanges of views, and to move participants towards agreed statements on areas of concern and on possible 'criteria' for monitoring.

The facilitator commented that:

> In these three workshops, several sets of issues have been defined, each within a slightly different conceptual framework and investigative procedure. Each is of interest in its own right, and the similarities, overlaps and differences between them are also of interest. It might moreover be of interest to look at them cumulatively as an instance of 'progressive focusing of issues' of the sort favoured by some exponents of illuminative evaluation. (Beattie 1993)

The issues were the ones which students and part-time staff were concerned about. Insights from this type of qualitative approach do give a good idea of the range of issues which are of concern to students and to part-time staff. Some aspects which were the cause of concern included:

- the size and frequency of tutorial groups;
- access to buildings for the disabled;
- extended waiting period before exam resit could be taken;
- late arrival of materials;
- quantity of written material received(!)

This information will be used to develop a regular systematic feedback questionnaire. Transforming the qualitative feedback into a structured instrument provides an accurate idea of the extent and degree to which the issues identified from the qualitative study are shared concerns among students and staff; and to establish their relative importance.

The three approaches each produced a rather different type of information. It is necessary to be clear about the type of information required before deciding how to go about gathering it. In a sense, the strategies used in the examples were attempting to do two different tasks. One was the identification of individual problems in order to take action and rectify any organizational errors. The other was to identify broader problems, both one-off, due to some specific cause, or endemic, where the system itself was revealed as inadequate. It would depend very much on what your major concerns were as to which one, or which combination of strategies you should choose as the most appropriate for your situation.

Chapter 7

Developing your own programme evaluation system

In this chapter, we will be focusing on the first stage in designing and setting up a programme evaluation system. We will be considering the major issues on which decisions have to be taken including the purposes of the system, the providers of the service, the policies which shape it, and possible priority setting mechanisms.

One of the main temptations in any evaluation activity is to give the question of *how* you might approach the problem more attention than the question of *what* the problem is really about. In other words, time and effort have to be spent on the process of identifying and clarifying exactly what problem you are trying to solve. Peter Drucker put it succinctly when he said that 'the important and difficult job is never to find the right answer, it is to find the right question. For there are few things as useless – if not as dangerous – as the right answer to the wrong question' (Drucker 1979).

This is particularly true in respect of designing and setting up an evaluation system. In fact you may find it helpful to think of the development of an evaluation system as a three-phase process:

- Clarify what it is that you want the system to do, ie clarify the nature of the system, its purposes, policies and priorities.
- Work out how the system is going to be operated, in other words, how you are going to achieve the agreed purposes of the system.
- Establish how you are going to know whether you are achieving those purposes, or whether the system needs to be modified in some way.

In this chapter we will be focusing on the first of these phases, with the other phases being discussed in the final two chapters.

The purpose of your evaluation system

During the first phase of the development of a programme evaluation system, that is when you are clarifying its purposes, there are three basic questions which need to be considered:

- What are the aims and objectives of the evaluation system?
- What will be its major areas of concern?
- Who will be its clients?

The questions listed here are not necessarily the only questions that you might ask or even the best questions for your situation, but in getting the answers to them, you will be able to identify other questions which might be particularly relevant for your own situation.

Aims and objectives of the evaluation system

The primary aim of any organizational system in overall terms is to help the organization to achieve its aims and objectives. The question which has to be considered in respect of a specific system is what is its particular contribution to the achievement of these aims and objectives? There are a number of different ways you might wish to answer this. A list of the objectives of a programme evaluation system for an open and distance learning organization might include some of the following:

- to monitor progress towards stated organizational goals;
- to support the promotion of the quality of teaching;
- to help monitor and control academic standards;
- to help monitor and control standards of teaching, student services and student support;
- to support the expansion of the provision without loss of quality;
- to help improve the standards of teaching, student services and student support;
- to help improve the appropriateness of the provision for students.

These objectives are not intended to be mutually exclusive or exhaustive. They are intended to give you a feel for the types and range of objectives which an evaluation system may be called upon to hold. It may be that the major purpose of the system relates to aspects of control and accountability.

Or it may be that you intend it to have a more developmental role. Whatever the detailed objectives, the view expressed by Wilbur Schramm some years ago admirably sums up the overall aim of any evaluation system, namely that its aim should be to provide information which will 'decrease the uncertainty within which education has to be designed, materials prepared and learners to learn' (Schramm 1977).

What will be its major areas of concern?

You may decide, for example, that your evaluation system should only focus on the students themselves – who they are, their retention and their success rates. Or you might wish to extend the activities covered by evaluation and include students' interaction with teaching materials, or with the personal support they receive, or the face-to-face teaching. The list below might be helpful as a prompt and to check which areas of activities you might wish to include within your own system.

- Students: demographic profile; academic performance, access to course components.
- Recruitment of students.
- Learning effectiveness of new media.
- Face-to-face teaching.
- Student use of and response to course materials.
- Design, development and modification of course materials.
- Student assessment.
- Student support and information.

In determining the extent of the coverage of the evaluation system, you will have to take into account the resources available and the constraints under which the system may have to operate.

You will also need to identify the particular focus which it would be most appropriate for your evaluation system to adopt. For example, suppose you are working with a small open learning unit (OLU) which is seen very much as a pilot scheme by its sponsors. You know that in, say, three years the unit will be subject to a major review. Clearly the OLU will be concerned to present evidence of its achievements up to that point. This would indicate the need for a summative focus. At the same time, however, evidence of the presence of an evaluation system within the ULO which provided formative information and agreed procedures for implementing changes informed by that information would also be seen as desirable by those carrying out the review.

A rather different example might be an OLU which is growing rapidly and which needs information and advice about the best way of modifying its training programme structure and about transforming courses it has bought in so that they meet the needs of the corporate customers and the students more closely. A formative focus would be needed here for an evaluation system. However, summative judgements about aspects of the structure and of the courses would need to be made as part of the process of determining which courses needed most attention and which aspects of the programme structure needed modifying.

Clients

It may be tempting to argue that an evaluation system should cover as many of the organization's activities as possible. But this is not necessarily the most appropriate approach. One of the problems, as we saw in an earlier chapter, is that any organization, but especially one involved with open and distance teaching, will consist of different but interconnected systems. The question you have to resolve is how much of each and how many of them it is feasible to attempt to cover through the evaluation system. Remember, you may still have clients who are members of systems which are not included within the evaluation system.

The next issue therefore concerns the question of who you see as the major clients or users of the work of the evaluation system. While the students or the corporate customers or the funding agencies may be the beneficiaries of the evaluation work, the clients of the evaluation system are those people whom it is intended will make direct use of its services. Within an open and distance teaching organization, possible clients might be:

- senior management within the organization;
- programme heads;
- course designers;
- selected committees;
- student representatives;
- tutors.

The groups you identify as potential clients will, to a large extent, depend on the decision-making structure you have within your organization. For example, a hierarchical structure will have different decision-making procedures to one with a more democratic structure, or one which operates devolved decision-making. The point is that the appropriate decision-makers must be among the groups identified as the major clients of the system.

The intended nature of your evaluation system

The question of who will actually provide the evaluation service (in the sense of carrying out the evaluation studies) and how they are intended to operate is one which you might need to consider when you are clarifying the purposes of the evaluation system. There are three different models which can be adopted in considering who will be designing and carrying out the evaluation work. Evaluation studies may be:

1 Externally designed and carried out.
2 Internally designed and carried out.
3 Some combination of 1 and 2.

The traditional model for educational innovations is probably the one which is externally designed and carried out. The assumption is frequently made that the advantage of this model is that an external evaluator will bring objectivity to the research task. However, the real strength of this model lies in the variety of skills and experience which different external experts can bring with them to the task.

Going for a model which is internally designed and carried out has the advantages of facilitating longer-term work, responsiveness to short-term needs, continuity, comparability and the incorporation of greater knowledge about the institution, its personalities and its power and decision-making structures.

The particular advantages of having some form of mixed provision depends on the form of the mix which you decide upon. This could range from, say, internal provision of design and coordination, with all research activities carried out by external consultants, to almost all design and research carried out internally, with external consultants occasionally brought in as an additional resource for a specific piece of research. Alternatively, external consultants could be brought in to design the evaluation studies, with internal staff actually carrying them out (see Figure 7.1).

Realistically, there will always be some internal evaluation work carried out. If there is none officially, then there will be some which is carried out unofficially. Management, teaching and support staff always need some form of feedback on their work, however rough and ready, to help their decision-making. In the long run, a core of work carried out internally is essential. The questions which each individual organization must answer are what is the appropriate size of that core and what resources can be committed to it?

	Design of studies	
Operation of studies	External Staff	Internal Staff
External Staff	✓	✓
Internal Staff	✓	✓

Figure 7.1 *Possibilities for provision of the evaluation service*

The basis on which those who carry out the evaluation will operate will also vary with and be an integral part of the purpose of the evaluation system. The list below shows some of the different bases on which programme evaluation can be organized.

- Participative evaluation.
- Self-evaluation.
- Self-evaluation with advice from expert.
- Expert evaluation.

Participative evaluation
Participative evaluation within an institution has the advantages and the disadvantages of the democratic approach to evaluation. The general approach is derived from the work of community action groups, but is transferable to many settings. Stephen Brookfield describes it as the turning of research exercises into activities

> in which the distinctions between researchers and subjects are blurred, to select topics for research according to subjects' definitions of importance, and to make data collection and data analysis a collaborative exercise in which all are involved in exploring and interpreting the multiple realities of subjects' perceptions. In participatory research, projects are conceived, designed, and conducted by the community for the benefit of all community members. (Brookfield 1986)

What Brookfield is saying is that the research is very much a joint exercise right through from deciding what needs to be investigated to agreeing what the findings are and what conclusions can be drawn from them. This approach does deal with the concern and even suspicion often felt by those whose activities are to be evaluated. However, it can be a slow process and external authorities may have to be convinced of the validity of conclusions drawn from work which has used this approach.

Self-evaluation

We saw in Chapter 4 how the individual projects which were part of the Open Tech Programme were all expected to organize and carry out their own evaluations. If the detailed evaluation of individual courses is seen as particularly important by the course designers or the programme manager, it might be seen as appropriate for course designers to carry out a self-evaluation. The advantage of this approach is that the course designers can make sure that any aspects they are particularly worried about are followed up. They are also 'in control' of the evaluation and of the findings.

Self-evaluation with advice from an expert

Self-evaluation with advice from an expert in evaluation or in research methods might be relatively routinized, taking the form of self-evaluation using template questionnaires for example, prepared by evaluation experts. Alternatively it might involve a special study investigating an aspect of particular concern, with the expert giving advice and guidance. This guidance may be given as and when requested, or it may be a condition laid down by the organization as a way of maintaining standards.

Expert evaluation

Expert evaluation has the advantage of being a resource which can be available to the whole organization. The major disadvantage is probably that of clients' expectations within the organization being too great for the resources available, with too many demands on what must inevitably be a relatively limited resource. An internal expert resource to provide the evaluation service does have many advantages. Probably some of the most telling are the opportunity to ensure that a basic common core of work is carried out and the opportunity both to win the confidence of those whose activities are the focus of the evaluation, and of acquiring and using 'insider' knowledge in the formulation of evaluation objectives and in their interpretation.

Realistically, the optimum basis for operating an evaluation system is likely to be through a mix of expert evaluation and self-evaluation advised by experts. The amount and the duration of funding available for the system and the personalities (and possibly prejudices) of the decision-makers will determine where the emphasis lies.

The need for clear evaluation policies

The aim of any policies on evaluation which you develop will be to provide a framework within which short-and medium-term decisions can be taken. The clarity, consistency and coherence of the plans for the development and operation of your evaluation system will depend to a large extent on the quality of the policies which you develop. For example, suppose your organization wants to evaluate the efficiency of its central administration. Is this a piece of work you would expect your evaluation system to undertake, or to make a contribution to? Or again, suppose your organization was thinking of introducing a self-evaluation policy, to be undertaken by all departments. What contribution, if any, would you expect to make?

Charles Handy points out in *The Age of Unreason* that 'The most difficult of policy decisions concern what and who belongs in the core [of an organization], what activities and which people.' (Handy 1990). Handy was making this point in relation to the idea of a 'Shamrock' organization, which would consist of three parts: a core, a contracted-out area of work, and work undertaken by temporary and part-time staff. As we saw earlier in the chapter, this combination of different types of contributions is one which applies also to a particular system, in this instance the evaluation system, within an organization.

Many organizations carry out ad hoc evaluations from time to time. The problem is that they need not necessarily add up to any sort of coherent whole. For example, senior management may ask for a certain course to be evaluated because they have received complaints from students; for a particular policy to be evaluated because it has long-term cost implications, and for a study of successful students to be undertaken in order to use the findings as supportive evidence in an external review of the organization's activities. All these are worthy activities, but together they add up to no more than they do separately.

The advantage of an evaluation *system* is that the research carried out within it can be organized to add up to more than the sum of the individual parts. What you are doing in effect, is deciding how much continuous system monitoring you are going to build in, and what the balance between continuous monitoring and ad hoc studies should be. This means that systems within different organizations are likely to be very different. As we have seen, their purposes may differ, their client groups may differ, and their nature may differ. By nature, I mean the character, the quality, the essential essence of the system. The evaluation system may be primarily geared to formative work or to summative work or to some combination of the two.

The balance between the two approaches will depend on the history and ethos of the institution for which you are designing the system.

If you think of the situation in your own organization, you will no doubt be able to identify areas where the organizational policy has been developed and other areas where as yet there is no policy. In practice, in any organization, the areas for which policies have been developed will tend to depend on the interests and concerns of the decision-makers.

When it comes to policies on evaluation therefore, the situation is likely once more to vary very much among institutions. Some will have no policies at all on evaluation while others will have developed at least a few. It should be recognized that it is a long, slow business. Even my own institution which has been carrying out evaluation work for almost 25 years is still developing evaluation-related policies.

So what should your evaluation policies look like? What issues should they cover? My list would include such topics as:

- the role and purpose of evaluation within the organization;
- clients to be served by evaluation;
- confidentiality of evaluation data;
- 'ownership' of evaluation data;
- quality of research work;
- demands on staff and students for data;
- how responsibility for evaluation is to be exercised within the organization;
- how evaluation is to be funded and resourced within the organization.

There will be many other issues, but the ones listed seem to occur as possible problem areas quite frequently.

Options for agreeing evaluation priorities

The determination of evaluation priorities and the establishment of appropriate mechanisms to select them is one of the most difficult of the organizational tasks for an evaluation system. (By 'priorities' I mean the ordering of choice on an agreed basis.) An example in the evaluation area might be if you were faced with the choice of either carrying out some research into the course choice issue, or carrying out some work on course feedback for a new course which was just being introduced. The question would be which of the two pieces of work you should tackle first. Who would make the decision and on what basis?

Why is there a need to establish priorities? The simplest answer is that they are needed in situations where, for whatever reason, choices have to be made. The classic example which springs to mind is the injunction 'women and children first' when evacuating a sinking ship. In other words, in a situation where there has to be an ordering, the basis of that ordering will establish the priority. In the lifeboat situation, if the commonly agreed priority based on gender and age did not exist, then a *de facto* priority would emerge, probably based on size and strength. In the example of the question about which evaluation work should be given priority, the *de facto* priority could be based on say the personal preferences of the evaluator, or the status of the client. In other words, where there is no formal agreed basis for establishing priorities, then other informal bases will be used. The advantages of having a clearly agreed formal basis for establishing evaluation priorities are that they can be public, and that once having agreed them, time and arguments can be saved by their continued use as the basis of ordering.

So how should priorities be selected and who should be doing the selection? The first question you need to ask of your organization is whether it has its own clear institutional priorities. If it does have clear agreed priorities, then identified evaluation needs can be matched against the institutional priorities. If it does not have priorities clearly stated, then there will be considerable problems in deciding which issues and problems should be tackled and in what order.

Whether or not your organization has clear priorities, it is likely that you will still need to agree some form of priority-setting procedure for the evaluation system. There are a whole variety of ways in which you might go about this exercise, but the aim is clear: you will need to emerge with a flexible set of priorities which can be used to determine what evaluation activities take place and when. In Figure 7.2 I identify four different approaches to the question of who identifies the evaluation priorities and how.

Each of these options has advantages and disadvantages. The relative importance of those advantages and disadvantages will depend very much on the type of organization within which you are setting up the evaluation system.

Empowered individual

For Option 1, the individual who is empowered to make the decisions about priorities on behalf of the organization would have to have a clear understanding of the needs of the organization, and hold sufficient status within it to be able to justify these decisions at the highest level. If the

1	Individual on behalf of the institution	initiates and/or responds to requests as and when made.
2	Individual in association with key others	interaction between individual and key others.
3	Advisory Committee	initiates and/or responds to requests at regular intervals.
4	Clients	commission work on a full-cost basis.

Figure 7.2 *Four approaches to determining evaluation priorities*

organization had no clear set of priorities, the criteria such a person would use would include the perceived benefits to the organization, the relative importance of the topic and the issues it embraced, and the extent to which the use of available resources could be optimized. The major disadvantages of this approach are that the findings from work initiated by that individual would not be 'owned' by anyone else; and that the priorities could be susceptible to modification for reasons other than those which were in the organization's best interests.

Individual together with key others

In Option 2, the individual would combine with key others to identify the priorities. An initial listing could be revised after comments from the key others and could be relatively easily and regularly updated. The advantages of this approach would be the shared understanding of the organization's needs for evaluation, and wider 'ownership' of the results of the studies on completion. One of the disadvantages would be problems of reconciling disagreements between the recommendations of the key others. To operate effectively, this group would have to be relatively small.

Advisory Committee

Option 3 is the Advisory Committee approach. In theory this approach has a number of benefits. It can ensure representation of the key clients, and discussion of competing demands. In practice, the value of the approach is limited by the availability of the members for meetings and the resources they can call upon to supplement the core funding available for evaluation.

The commissioning clients

Finally, Option 4 is an approach which is used in many organizations. Its main advantage is that the clients feel in control over what work is done and when. The relevance of the evaluation activities to their immediate needs is clear. However, the major drawbacks are that the level of demand can vary considerably, that the problems clients want addressed are often short term in nature, and that the totality of work being commissioned by different clients does not necessarily add up to an efficient system as far as the organization as a whole is concerned.

Clearly there are many other ways in which an organization can go about setting its priorities. There may be a number of different approaches used in the same organization. In fact, all four methods were in use at the same time in one organization I worked with (for different areas of evaluation activity). What is important is that whatever the method used, the balance of priorities between the main types of activities must be clear to those who have to organize the evaluation work. What should be the proportion of resources committed to long-term as opposed to short-term issues; which of the different topic areas such as course design, student support, student services, component mix, programme policy, curriculum planning, have what priority; what should be the balance between formative and summative work and which clients should receive what priority?

Conclusion

If you are planning to introduce your own programme evaluation system, you should by this point have:

- identified the aims and objectives of the system;
- defined the major client(s) for the products of the system;
- established the nature of the system – who provides the service, the major policies, and how priorities are going to be established.

You should now be ready to consider how you are going to achieve the purposes for which the evaluation system is being established. In the next chapter, we will go through the activities and decisions which need to be undertaken in order to achieve the agreed purposes of the evaluation system.

Chapter 8

Organizing your programme evaluation system

In this chapter we will be looking at the second of the phases in the development of an evaluation system. We will be looking at the issues you need to consider in order to work out how the system is going to be operated, the different sorts of methodologies and research instruments that you can choose to use, the need to establish the extent of provision already available through the system, the resources you will need and your timetable for implementation.

Research tools and methodologies

An example

An extensive and multidimensional evaluation project was set up involving a number of linked projects examining the experiences and reactions not only of students but also of the academics who developed the course materials, computing support staff, local tutors and other staff. The data-collecting tools of the evaluation were large-scale student surveys, student journals and interviews with staff and students . . .

The survey questionnaires contained multiple-choice questions which were analysed using SPSS software on a Sperry Univac mainframe computer. They also contained open-ended questions which were an excellent source for understanding patterns of student use between courses and the open-ended responses were most useful in identifying the detailed nature of particular course issues and problems. A much smaller number of telephone and face-to-face interviews were carried out, fewer than the evaluation team would have ideally liked but the time-consuming nature of interviewing a nationally distributed population meant that the team were able to carry out very few. Journals, although in theory very attractive since they could provide a longitudinal study of student experience at low cost to the evaluator, proved in practice to have a low completion rate by students. However, those students who did return them provided another source of useful information and opinion which was incorporated with the other evaluation data. (Jones, Kirkup and Kirkwood 1992).

This extract is from a book which describes in some detail a major three-year evaluation study. The innovation the authors were involved in evaluating was the introduction of a home-computing policy by the Open University which required 17,000 students on different courses to acquire and use PCs at home as an official component of their course. The reason I have included details of the evaluation approach adopted by the evaluation team is because it illustrates very well the range of research tools and methodologies which may need to be called upon in the course of a major study. Let me summarize the component parts of the study:

Respondents

- Students.
- Academics who developed the course materials.
- Computing support staff.
- Local tutors.
- Other staff.

The data-collecting tools

- Large-scale student surveys containing both closed and open questions.
- Student journals.
- Telephone interviews.
- Face-to-face interviews.

The student statistics research data-base was also used to provide comparative data for investigating the equal opportunities aspects of the policy as a key part of the overall evaluation.

Multiple data sources, multiple usage

The study described above was funded as a special exercise because of the important long-term pedagogic, resource and institutional implications of the particular policy being implemented. The design reflected the complexity of the issues being addressed. However, it is not only the evaluations of major innovations which need to draw on a range of different sources of data.

For example, the evaluation of a particular course could draw not only from any study specifically designed to get detailed feedback on that course, but also on student demographic data, student progress and performance data, and data from any comparative course feedback studies which have been carried out. Conversely, as Figure 8.1 shows, data collected from individual studies can be used for a variety of different purposes, with data from a number of different studies contributing to the investigation of a particular issue, thus optimizing their usefulness.

The studies which form the framework of the evaluation system therefore need to be selected carefully. This set of studies should be sufficiently flexible to allow for growth and development in a way which will reflect the issues, concerns and priorities of the future. With any particular study, the methodology adopted will to some extent be constrained by the time available for carrying out the work, the costs involved, the methodological expertise and the support staff available.

Types of studies used for evaluation activities

What types of study should be considered for inclusion in your evaluation system? There are a range of different types of studies which can provide the data needed for the evaluation programme (see Figure 8.2).

Of the studies detailed here, some use secondary data, some are routine monitoring studies, while others may be more appropriate as occasional ad hoc studies.

Statistical studies from research data-base

As has been pointed out, most open and distance teaching organizations already collect some data on their students. This data can provide a rich source of information for your programme evaluation system. Accurate student data underpins the evaluation system, so there are strong arguments for locating responsibility for the production, interpretation and dissemination of statistical data studies in one place.

Issues for Evaluation	Student Demographic Profile	Student Progress and Performance	Assignment Submission and Grade Distribution Profiles	Monitoring of feedback on Assignments	Activity Monitoring	Environmental Monitoring	External Population Studies	Student Feedback	Staff Feedback	Comparative Course Feedback	Course Specific Studies	Feasibility Studies	Policy/System Reviews
Feasibility of programme/course	✓						✓	✓				✓	
Effectiveness of programme	✓	✓	✓	✓	✓		✓	✓	✓	✓			
Evaluation of courses	✓	✓	✓	✓	✓								
Component effectiveness				✓	✓	✓			✓	✓	✓		
Student Support	✓	✓	✓	✓				✓	✓	✓	✓		
Student Assessment	✓	✓	✓	✓		✓		✓			✓		✓
Course Development					✓		✓				✓	✓	
Course Production and Delivery								✓	✓				
Regional Support					✓			✓	✓				
Awareness						✓	✓					✓	
Enquiries	✓							✓					
Applications	✓	✓	✓					✓					
Testing	✓	✓	✓					✓					
Entry	✓	✓	✓	✓									
Preparation	✓												
Non-Acceptance								✓			✓		
Induction	✓	✓			✓			✓	✓		✓		
Data Audit	✓	✓	✓	✓	✓	✓	✓	✓	✓	✓	✓	✓	✓

Figure 8.1 *Ranges of data required for different types of study*
Source: © J. Calder, OU 1992

Statistical studies from research data-base
1 Student demographic profiles
2 Student progress and performance data
3 Assignment submission and grade distribution profiles

Regular monitoring studies
1 Assessors' feedback on assignments monitoring
2 Face-to-face activities monitoring
3 Environmental monitoring
4 External population studies
5 Student feedback studies
6 Staff feedback studies
7 Course feedback – comparative studies

Ad hoc studies
1 Course specific evaluations
2 Feasibility studies
3 Policy/system reviews

Figure 8.2 *Studies which might be included in your programme evaluation*

Student demographic profiles

Examples of basic demographic student profiles are those which show the aggregate distributions of the total student population across the major socio-economic or occupation variables by cohort of entry. They can also show the major socio-economic variables analysed by programme, by course and by region or geographic area where appropriate.

The tables produced should give both absolute figures and percentages. Some commentary can be provided to draw attention to the main items of interest, major trends and possible areas of concern. If you have phased entry, then the feasibility of developing student demographic profiles for each phase for applicants, entrance test examinees, those who pass the entrance test, non-acceptors and acceptors could be investigated.

Student progress and performance data

A student progress and performance monitoring system can identify problem stages or problem events for students. A basic measure of the success of any programme is whether or not students successfully complete the series of courses which comprise the programme. The numbers of registered students sitting exams and their subsequent results can be

Annual data

1   For the organization or unit as a whole and for each programme:
- the distribution of number of credits achieved for that year and cumulatively since entry for each entry cohort;
- size and sequence of drop-down in numbers between initial enquiry and acceptance of a place;
- the numbers and percentages of students registering with the organization that year, submitting assignments, applying for exams, sitting the exams and passing exams.

2   At the course level:
- the submission and success rates of students on each course analysed by cohort of entry and by other major demographics.

- Routine course-based statistics should include:
    - Exam attendance and pass rates.
    - Number of credits awarded by cohort.
    - Correlation between entrance test results and subsequent course success.
    - Pattern of course completion and credit awards.

Figure 8.3 *Student progress and performance data*

routinely disseminated to those areas within the organization involved in course and programme design, development and support. The range of issues which this data informs is as wide as that for student demographic data. Student progress and performance data can be made available at each of three levels of detail: organizational, programme and course (see Figure 8.3).

Such sets of analyses can then be routinely distributed to key individuals and groups such as course teams, senior management, major committees and any relevant sub-units. Similarly the numbers and percentages of registered students entering for exams together with exam results can be presented and circulated for consideration annually, in a common format, for all courses. The question of how best to monitor findings from these data and what actions should be taken as a result of problems identified will need to be decided. The aim would be to identify an effective way of ensuring maximum utilization of the data.

Assignment and grade distribution profiles
- the distribution of number of assignments submitted by course and by programme;
- the distribution of grades awarded by course within programme, across programmes, by study centre, region, and for the major demographics such as gender and qualification status;
- a distribution of grades awarded by assessors for each assignment would assist the development of the moderation system;
- the percentages submitting each assignment and the success rates for each course on a cohort basis.

Figure 8.4 *Assignment submission and grade distribution profiles*

Assignment submission and grade distribution profiles

These profiles contribute to the investigation of as large a number of issues as the two previous statistical studies. In particular they contribute to evaluations of programme effectiveness, course evaluations, and evaluations of student support and student assessment. This can be achieved by designing the profiles shown in Figure 8.4.

Cohort data for each programme should also show the distribution of accumulated credits on an annual basis, with cross-breaks by major student demographics. These results should be presented in a common format for all courses to facilitate comparisons. Again, consider who should routinely receive such data.

Regular monitoring studies

Some studies will be needed which operate regularly and routinely, building up data-bases over time and enabling trends to be tracked and comparisons to be made. Seven types of monitoring studies are listed in Figure 8.2. Once designed and operating, they would require only minor modifications during regular operation.

Assessors' feedback on assignments monitoring

The monitoring of feedback sheets received by students from assessors contributes to course evaluations (through the identification of the problems being experienced by students), to the evaluation of the support received by students, and to the evaluation of the quality of student assessment. The mechanisms for selecting, say, a 2 per cent sample of assessor feedback on assignments on all courses will need to be introduced if they do not already exist, with copies of selected assessor feedback going to the tutors or to the individuals holding continuing responsibility for the teaching quality of the course. This data can be reviewed and synthesized to identify the most and least successful aspects of each part of the course. This could be used to brief and advise assessors and tutors for the coming year on the sort of help which students were most likely to need. It could also be used in revising the course at the appropriate time.

Face-to-face activities monitoring

Any face-to-face activities are likely to benefit from routine monitoring. In particular, the need for feedback from such activities as induction meetings, residential schools and study centre activities should be reviewed. The feedback can be of two types: the routine completion of simple feedback sheets by participants after involvement in any event can be used at the local level to improve presentation and organization of activities; at the same time some monitoring of such activities could be carried out centrally. This can be based in part on a sample of the routine local feedback but the need to supplement it by specially devised monitoring studies from the centre should be considered.

Environmental monitoring

Environmental monitoring provides the organization with information which can be used for comparative and contextual purposes. In particular, there may be the following information needs:

- courses offered by other similar organizations;
- pass rates at other organizations;
- costs at other organizations;
- new developments in distance teaching;
- new developments in non-formal adult provision nationally.

The responsibility for identifying the key areas, for ensuring that the work is carried out to a satisfactory standard and for the work to be accessible to all members of the organization who need this data for their decision-making needs to be clearly located.

External population studies

If you wish to build up a picture of the extent and nature of public awareness of your organization, then commercial market research companies who undertake omnibus surveys may well be the most cost-effective solution. If your public is primarily within a corporate organization, then you may want to consider carrying out your own awareness study. A set of appropriate questions on recognition of the unit's or organization's name and on knowledge of its special features would need to be devised. The data from such surveys will need interpretation and dissemination and again, responsibility for this aspect would need to be assigned.

Studies which investigate in more detail the interface between the general public and the organization can also be included here. Sample surveys of people who have enquired but have not applied and of people who applied but who chose not to accept the offer of a place will need to be undertaken. The importance of these issues to the organization should be included in the reviews of evaluation priorities.

Student feedback studies

One difficulty with open and distance learning programmes which can often arise can be in distinguishing between those students who are

---

Student feedback studies

Students' study plans: A student survey which investigates and monitors students' study plans, expectations, motives, goals, preparation for study, study circumstances and access to study facilities. Can be undertaken on an annual basis. In particular, it should address any issues such as the period of time over which students plan to study for their qualification; and the range and extent of timetabling and pacing problems which students are encountering.

Student satisfaction surveys: These are studies which are used to monitor students' satisfaction with the organization. Issues covered can range from course choice, and access problems to response times for information and queries and for feedback from tutors on assignments. These surveys are primarily used for feedback on students' study experience, and problems with and treatment by the system.

Non-completing students surveys: Students who registered for a course, but who do not complete the assessment component can be followed up to monitor and investigate their reasons for non-completion. This type of student may well be disaffected and there can be particular problems of non-response associated with gathering information from them.

Figure 8.5 *Student feedback studies*

studying at their own pace; those who are temporarily 'resting' but who intend to continue with their studies, and those who have, to all intents and purposes given up. The records may indicate only those students who are currently active in that they have submitted the most recent assignment. It may therefore be necessary to collect information about students' plans for study via student surveys.

Student survey data could also usefully establish any variability among courses, programmes, cohorts and major demographic groupings.

Staff feedback studies

Feedback from counsellors, assessors, tutors and other support staff on their attitudes to and experience of the teaching, delivery and support systems can also be gathered on a regular basis. In addition, their views on the relevance of the curriculum to learners' needs, and their attitudes towards distance teaching could be monitored through the same survey.

Course feedback – comparative studies

A comparative overview study of course feedback on courses would examine student response on issues such as workload, difficulty levels, whether the material was motivating, use of and reactions to components including support from counsellors, problems with language and so on. This might be a routine periodic study with the findings reported to those responsible for course development and course presentation. Any courses identified as having particular problems could be followed up in more detail through course specific evaluation studies (see below).

Ad hoc studies

As the number of routine studies builds up, there will be a matching growth in demand for ad hoc studies. In part, this is because the routine studies will themselves raise as many questions as they answer. In part, members of the organization will become accustomed to having access to reliable data which can inform their decision-making.

Course specific evaluations

While summative forms of course evaluation may on occasion be necessary, formative course evaluations will be more helpful to you for improving the quality of the courses which you offer to students. Because of the cost of this type of evaluation, courses should be selected for evaluation because of known difficulties or because they are innovative in some particular way. In-depth feedback can be designed to give detailed information about student problems at unit or block level. A variety of methodologies are available, with the most appropriate approach being determined by the nature of the type of problem being investigated.

Feasibility studies

Feasibility studies by their very nature must meet certain key conditions. Their timing must fit the programme's decision-making timetable; the issues they address must be comprehensive, and the studies need to be accurately targeted in relation to the potential student body for the course or programme. Feasibility studies should normally be carried out on an ad hoc basis; each being specially designed to meet the requirements of the course or programme being considered. Issues such as course aims, content, level, structure, length, pacing, workload and media utilization will all need to be addressed.

Policy/system reviews

It is in the nature of reviews and with major policy studies that their methodology and the location of responsibility for carrying them out will vary with the problem. On occasion, it may be necessary to involve external consultants. At other times, it may be more appropriate to commission internal members of staff. Clearly it is useful if reviews are carried out by someone who is familiar with the system and who has some knowledge of the detailed processes of the organization.

Organizing your system

Issues needing decisions

Actually setting up the system means that a number of decisions on key issues have to be made. In considering these issues, the question of the overall level of investment in programme evaluation must be considered. A good rule of thumb is to think of something of the order of 5 to 7 per cent of the total budget. However, where a major investment is being considered, the evaluation costs might well exceed this amount. Whatever the level of investment, however, decisions have to be taken about the management, staffing and resourcing of the evaluation activities.

Management responsibilities

Whatever the nature of the system which has been decided upon, the person managing the evaluation programme will need to develop a focal point, comprising either an individual or group of individuals, who will act as the central point for programme evaluation activities. Decisions will need to be taken about what the management responsibilities are. Whether they include, for example,

- coordination of current evaluation activities, concerns and interests of staff in different parts of the organization;
- devising and agreeing procedures for programme evaluation priorities;
- setting/advising on priorities for the evaluation programme and receiving reports on progress;
- advising on the level of resources which should be made available for evaluation activities;
- receiving reports of evaluation findings and recommendations and advising how their recommendations should be handled, and by whom.

Clearly many other areas of responsibility can be identified. The point is that management responsibilities should be clearly outlined at the outset.

Staffing

A commitment to a minimum level of staffing overall for evaluation work does need to be made, however modest. You may find that some areas may already be making allocations of staff time to evaluation activities. However, the level and duration of these commitments should be made explicit. Individuals with no formal responsibility for evaluation might still wish to carry out and participate in research and evaluation activities, and indeed this can be wholly desirable and beneficial. With the support of a properly resourced professional evaluation capacity, other departments or local units should be able to carry out a wide range of evaluation research specific to their own needs. At the same time it would clearly be necessary for all those engaging in evaluation to maintain close links with any core staff both to benefit from their advice and expertise, and to feed back their findings and conclusions to the documentation centre so that they would be available to the wider organization.

Necessary core staffing roles and expertise are likely to include:

- computing/statistical expertise for data management and presentation;
- survey design and management and evaluation methodology expertise to assist with the development, organization and analysis of major routine quantitative surveys of staff and students;
- administrative support to organize survey processing and analysis of questionnaires and interview tapes, and supervise clerical support;
- clerical support for survey handling and processing and data input.

Non-staff resources

Access to appropriate hardware and software for the holding of data files, construction of data-bases and the analysis of survey data will be needed. The computer analysis of survey data makes a tremendous difference in the time taken to complete surveys, in the quality of the analyses which can be undertaken, and in the number of studies which can be undertaken. A storage capacity of around 100 MB would enable large data-sets to be handled and major analysis software packages such as SPSS to be used. Laser printers would enable graphs and other forms of data presentation to be used and to print out data at speed.

Budget

There should preferably be a dedicated budget which allows for the sorts of costs listed in Figure 8.6. The organization may cover many costs automatically, but it should be ensured that resources are available to cover those listed.

- Dissemination costs – to cover such items as in-house publication, costs associated with putting on workshops, giving presentations of evaluation findings.
- Travel.
- Conference attendance.
- Cost of commissioning external agencies for aspects of work (eg data entry, interviewing).
- Costs associated with buying participation in any external surveys carried out by independent research agencies.
- Temporary staff and consultants.
- Printing, reproduction and postage costs for postal surveys.

Figure 8.6 *Sample budget heads for evaluation costs*

There are clearly some serious resource implications in the decision to develop a capacity for systematic programme evaluation. However, a phased approach to the development of a programme evaluation system can reduce the pain somewhat. This would mean the expenditure associated with the development of a programme evaluation system could also be phased over several years.

Timetable for implementation

The aim of the phased approach outlined in Figure 8.7 is to tackle those problems which are of fundamental importance to the good functioning of your open and distance learning provision and to its reputation, and to acquire and develop resources of data and skills which underpin the development of a strong reliable and sustainable evaluation system.

The main foci for the evaluation activities during the early stages of development of the evaluation system could be:

- *Research Documentation Database*: One of the first steps in setting up an evaluation system is to review what data is currently available, where it is located, and how it can be accessed. You might also think about the possibility of an audit of other data which may be relevant to your areas of concern and which may also be held in different places within the organization. It is often the case that studies might have been commissioned or carried out in the past on an ad hoc basis without the results being disseminated any further than the immediate client. Research and evaluation documents, reviews, reports and research instruments which have already been used within the organization represent a valuable resource. A data audit would establish whether or not there are any relevant research and evaluation documents, reports, and research instruments of studies which have been carried out in different parts of the organization. The construction of a data-base holding information about all such studies should be a priority.

In the short term – during the first year
- establish the documentation, information and intelligence function;
- design and pilot major baseline surveys of staff, students and courses;
- set up ad hoc local action research project.

In the medium term – two to five years
- start the production of regular student progress and performance data;
- develop, test and introduce the major routine studies;
- ad hoc studies.

In the longer term – say six years onwards
- increase emphasis on ad-hoc studies;
- external population studies;
- problem specific studies.

Figure 8.7 *Sample timetable for implementation*

- *Collation of existing statistical data:* Existing statistical data on student demographics, progress and performance on the different courses and programmes of study should be brought together, synthesized and systematically reviewed.
- *Review of programmes and issues presenting major problems:* Exam results and credit accumulation figures can be reviewed to identify the areas in which there may be a problem with student retention and success. The data should be reviewed to check if this issue or other issues appear to present the greater problems.

In the short term – during the first year, the focus for evaluation activities should be on identifying the major problem areas with regard to student retention and success and in setting up a basic evaluation infrastructure.

Given that the major problem areas had been identified during the first year and that the basic infrastructure for an evaluation system had been established, the focus could then move on to evaluation activities which would contribute to improving the student retention and success figures. The evaluation system itself should develop further and move into a relatively stable stage, with the main routine studies being developed and introduced.

Assuming acceptable levels of student retention and success are being achieved, the organization would be in a position to refocus its priorities for the evaluation system to include wider access and more choice of courses. By this stage, the evaluation system should be in a position to cope with a considerably wider range of studies.

Conclusion

The design and setting up of a system of programme evaluation is a complex task. In this chapter we have been looking at the options open to you for setting up a system which will achieve the purposes agreed for it. During the building up of that system, the growth in demands and in client expectations will present their own challenges. However, demand is not the only, or even the most reliable criterion of success. At some point, and the sooner the better if changes have to be made, you will need to review whether you are achieving the purposes for which the system was established and funded. In order to do this, you will need to establish for the system clear criteria by which its organization and its work can be reviewed. In the next chapter, we move on to the final stage in the development and operation of a system for programme evaluation, considering how best it can be made into a self-improving system.

Chapter 9

A self-improving system

This chapter covers the third and final phase in setting up a system of programme evaluation: the reviewing and development of your evaluation system. It discusses what sort of self-assessment will be appropriate in order for you to be able to review your own success in achieving the objectives you set for the system and it looks at the issues associated with undertaking this work, including identifying the stakeholders, planning the self-evaluation and carrying it out.

A self-improving system

The process of review and development is essential to the idea of a self-improving system. Just as the aim of your programme evaluation system is to help your own organization to meet its aims, both in terms of accountability and in terms of its development as a provider of open and distance learning, so the evaluation system also needs to be both account-able for its consumption of organizational resources and responsive to the need to develop as a system. It is therefore important to know whether you are achieving those purposes which your evaluation system was set up to tackle, or whether the system needs to be modified in some way.

An evaluation system, like any other system, needs to assess whether and to what extent it is meeting its aims. To do this it needs to monitor its activities and to take action on the findings. For example, take the case where external demands for accountability on the organization change the emphasis from judging institutional success by intake of students and provision of a wide range of courses to judging it by student success rates and employability. Here the type of data collected and the clients for that data within the organization might be expected to change somewhat, or at least be modified. For example, instead of focusing on evaluating access initiatives, or carrying out studies of enquirers who do not go on to apply for a course, priority would be given to follow-up studies of students who have completed their course, or the monitoring of student drop-out, or the investigation of the causes of student drop-out from different courses where levels appear to be unacceptably high. Different sorts of studies might well need different types of professional expertise, or different ways of working.

What we are in effect talking about is the self-evaluation of the evaluation system. In order to do this, you need to consider the following issues.

- Who is going to be involved and in what way?
- What are the questions which have to be asked?
- How and when is the self-evaluation going to be done?
- What are the resourcing implications?

As with any other evaluation, the quality of the planning and design of the study will determine its ultimate usefulness. The difference is that this time, it is you and your system under the microscope. You may experience feelings of vulnerability or concerns about the extent to which the outcomes of the study will accurately represent what is going on. This can only be described as a valuable learning experience which will give some insight into or remind you about the feelings of those others in the organization whose activities are normally the focus of attention.

Who is going to be involved and in what way?

The process of self-evaluation for an organizational system is of its nature bound to involve people in a range of different ways. To be successful, it needs at least the participation, even if not the wholehearted enthusiasm, of those who carry out evaluation activities, and those who use the findings from them.

Ownership of the process

That the ownership of the process of self-evaluation is an issue may seem on the face of it a little odd. However the increasing practice of funders and accrediting bodies of demanding evidence that self-evaluation is carried out and often of requiring reports on the findings of self-evaluations means that what might in different circumstances be a private reflective process becomes a public event. The self-evaluation process might initially be triggered by demands external to the evaluation system or even external to the organization, or may be driven by the need to be seen to be operating such a process. The decision therefore has to be made at an early stage as to whether the ownership of the process lies:

- within the group of those who carry out evaluation activities;
- within some wider organizational framework; or
- external to the organization.

Ownership involves the determination of the aims and objectives of the system, the criteria of success, the standards and the norms and the conclusions drawn from the findings. Ownership centred within the evaluation system does not exclude the utilization of the self-evaluation data by others outside the system for whatever purposes they wish. It does, however, mean that any conclusions drawn from the self-evaluation process are more likely to be owned and therefore acted upon by those involved in the evaluation system.

Who is involved?

Some of the stakeholders in the self-evaluation of the evaluation system have already been mentioned. Those who actually organize and carry out evaluation activities can be seen as part of that system. Depending on the model operating within your institution, these people may be members of a small core with a substantial responsibility for evaluation activities, or they may be people, such as tutors or course team members, whose main responsibilities are elsewhere but who do occasionally undertake this type of work. At the same time, the users and the potential users of the evaluation findings will clearly have an interest in the self-evaluation. These may include external as well as internal users. Evaluation findings can be used in all sorts of unexpected ways and by a whole range of people with different organizational responsibilities. The problem here will lie in reviewing the groups who are to be seen as the primary clients of the programme evaluation system.

The possibility of involving one other group in the self-evaluation needs consideration. Students are approached for the purposes of obtaining information for the various evaluation studies which are undertaken and will also have views about the operation of the evaluation system as it affects them. The quality and reliability of evaluation work depends to a considerable extent on the willingness and cooperation of the students, or former students, to spend time and effort in feeding back information about themselves and in giving their views and opinions. The size and extent of the demands which evaluation activities make on them will need to be addressed in some way as part of the review of any evaluation system.

Roles of those involved

The review will have to be planned, organized, controlled and coordinated. Its findings will have to be interpreted and finally reported and acted upon. The focus on self-evaluation suggests that the allocation of the major roles should be with the knowledge and agreement of those whose work is included in the evaluation.

Responsibility for the review

The key question initially will be who should take overall responsibility for the self-evaluation: the person or people who control the work and who stand as guarantors that the work will be carried out to the agreed standard within the specified period of time and within the resources allocated. That person should also stand as guarantor of the use to which the findings will be put. Those who contribute to the self-evaluation will need to know and have confidence that the reason given for carrying out the work is the one to which it will be put. The person who takes on that role could be anyone who has the confidence of those who carry out evaluation work and possibly also those who use its findings. The latter group are important in that they will have to contribute to the evidence which will be collected as part of the self-evaluation process. They may also be the recipients of the evaluation findings. The individual who takes on the responsibility for the self-evaluation process may be:

- the person responsible for the evaluation system;
- one of the people who carry out evaluation activities;
- a user of evaluation findings; or
- someone external to the evaluation process.

Clearly each of these possibilities has advantages and disadvantages depending in part on the organizational context in which you are operating and in part on the particular individuals concerned and their acceptability to the stakeholders in the self-evaluation.

Dissemination

The question of the dissemination of the findings can be crucial to the success of the self-evaluation. The question of how much of the findings, in what form, and to whom they should be circulated needs to be addressed at an early stage. Who should know the full findings? Should there be separate in-house and public documents? Whose authority and agreement should be given before the circulation of any findings? In part these issues will be affected by the amount and type of experience staff have in regard to self-evaluation. They will also be affected by the extent to which self-evaluation which has been set up for development purposes has also to serve summative or accountability purposes.

Reviewing or judging

The question of who takes on the role of interpreting the findings and making judgements on them again needs to be determined at an early stage. If the review is seen primarily as a within-system formative review, and particularly if it is an ongoing activity, then the judgements about the implications of the findings for the way in which the evaluation system operates might be seen as a purely internal affair. However, if the findings suggest that changes to the structure, organization or resourcing of the system are needed, then clearly the findings will need to be made available to those responsible for such decision-making in order that they may assess the findings as evidence of the need for any recommended changes.

What are the questions which have to be asked?

The questions to be asked will probably be related to one or more of the following:

- Aims and objectives of the system.
- Relevance of issues tackled to organizational priorities.
- Timeliness of reports.
- Appropriateness of dissemination strategies.
- Accessibility of findings.
- Utilization of findings.
- Perceived value for money.

The first step is therefore to clarify on which questions the self-evaluation should focus. The methodology to be used and the sources of the data which will be collected in order to provide answers to those questions will follow on from this step.

Aims and objectives of the system

You will need to establish whether or not clear aims and objectives for the evaluation system exist, and the extent to which participants in the evaluation process are aware of them and whether they agree with them. We discussed the different types of aims and objectives which an evaluation system might hold in Chapter 7. As the organization itself evolves and changes, its own aims and those of its component systems must also evolve and change.

Relevance of issues tackled to organizational priorities

If the organizational priorities are clearly expressed and regularly reviewed and updated, the matching of the issues tackled over a period of time within the evaluation system to those priorities should be relatively straightforward. Suppose for example that one of the organizational priorities is to broaden access to courses. Evaluation studies that might contribute to reviewing organizational progress with this priority might include monitoring of student demographics at entry and at later stages; the evaluation of any access initiatives organized or provided by the organization; building in an access dimension into the evaluation of courses by investigating any differential responses from different groups of students and so on. It is in looking for matches here that any major gaps in coverage or overlaps and possible areas of duplication of effort can also be identified.

Timeliness of reports

The matching of the timing of the reporting of evaluation findings to the decision-making timetable is the source of continuing tension in programme evaluation systems. Where there is only one primary client, the task is the relatively easy one of attempting to design and structure the evaluation study in such a way as to produce at least some basic findings in time to be used by the decision-makers. So, for example, a course evaluation can be designed and constructed in such a way as to feed back to the course tutors or the course designers or the course purchasers the summative or formative information that they need in order to make their decisions.

However, where there are multiple clients a somewhat greater difficulty presents itself. This is a particular problem with multi-purpose studies, and yet studies which can address a number of different issues at the same time can be an efficient and effective way of gathering data. Figure 8.1 on p 131 shows how most of the different types of studies do actually collect data which have multiple uses. The problem to be reviewed here may have to concentrate on getting priorities between the needs of different clients clearly agreed and the timetable for dissemination clearly spelt out and accepted.

Accessibility of findings

It can be easy to forget about the importance of access to evaluation findings. In Chapter 1 it was pointed out that the utilization of evaluation findings might frequently occur some considerable time after the initial study was carried out and disseminated (Westerheijden, Weusthof and Fredericks 1992). Unfortunately the more difficult it is to access the findings after their initial dissemination, the less likely it is that potential users will be able to utilize them at a later stage. Accessibility can refer to:

- physical access;
- content access; or
- quality access.

Physical access is a particular problem with decentralized evaluation systems. Data-sets, reports, or summaries of findings may well remain with the individual or group who carried out the evaluation study rather than being lodged in some central location. If reports or findings in whatever form are physically accessible, their contents may not be easily identified if only the title of the study is available. Similarly, in order for the relevance of the subjects and issues covered to be established, the appropriate level of detail about the coverage of the findings needs to be given. Finally, sufficient information has to be given about the methodology employed to establish the quality level of the data in terms of validity and reliability. Clearly the questions about the accessibility of evaluation findings are ones which both the users of evaluation findings and evaluators themselves need to consider.

Utilization of findings

This question is probably one of the most difficult for those involved in evaluation to answer. If there is no clear evidence that evaluation findings are utilized in some way, then two questions must be asked. First, what is it about the decision-making structure of the organization that results in what should be a source of key information to assist its decision-making being apparently disregarded? Second, what is it about the evaluation system or the way in which evaluation work is carried out which results in the lack of integration of evaluation findings and decision-making? Both these questions, however, presuppose that information on the nature and extent of organizational utilization of evaluation findings is collected.

Perceived value for money

To some extent this issue is linked to the question of the utilization of evaluation findings and, in fact, to the other questions before it. The major question for any organizational system has to be whether it gives that organization value for money. The phrase 'perceived value for money' is used for this section because the reality is that usually people make judgements on their perceptions of what is, rather than upon the actuality of what is. If the work of the evaluation system is not widely or if the full range of its activities is not clearly understood by those external to the system, then judgements about the value for money which it provides will unfortunately be based upon inadequate information. In order therefore to answer the question of value for money, it is first necessary to be clear about the evidence on which this assessment is to be made. The resource commitment of the organization to the evaluation system has to be clearly established, together with a clear analysis of the major sources of cost. The contribution of the the evaluation system to the processes and outcomes of the organization has also to be identified and documented. The subjective nature of much of this evidence is difficult to avoid. In spite of this, the costs of providing an 'in house' evaluation capacity as against such alternatives as 'buying in' expertise as and when required in order to achieve similar levels of contribution to the organization, do have to be investigated.

How and when is the self-evaluation to be done?

The question of the timing and frequency of self-evaluation activities is closely linked to the type of approach which is used for the exercise. Once the aims of the evaluation system have been identified and the areas of investigation have been agreed upon, then the next series of decisions about the self-evaluation have to be taken:

- What data are to be collected?
- What criteria should be used in assessing the data for evidence of success in achieving objectives?
- What is to be the coverage of the self-evaluation?
- What will be the sources of data and what means of collection will be used?
- What will be the frequency and duration of the self-evaluation?

We will now look at each of these issues in turn.

Types of data to be collected

The types of data to be collected will, to a large extent, vary with the issue being investigated. Let us suppose that one of the issues we are investigating is the timeliness of dissemination of findings with respect to users' needs.

We would first have to establish who the users were for a range of studies. A simple set of feedback information from those users would establish whether or not there were any grounds for concern from the users' perspective.

Even if they were quite satisfied, the opportunity might be taken to review whether the time allowed for meeting deadlines was over-generous. If there was some dissatisfaction among users with the timeliness or the quality of the presentation of findings, it might also be useful to establish what the formats were and what the timing was for the dissemination of the findings for each of those studies. Inevitably, the status or the perceived importance of the users will be used to weight their responses. The views of the chief executive or the principal will tend to be accorded greater weight than the views of other users, for example.

Other data which could be collected might include details of how deadlines were negotiated and clients' expectations with respect to timeliness. Examples of the different data which might be used for a range of issues related to the self-evaluation of an evaluation system will include regular quantitative feedback, special quantitative or qualitative studies, and impressionistic and subjective perceptions. The challenge is to be quite clear about the types of data you intend to use, and the reasons for having selected them.

What criteria should be used: aims, issues and types of data-criteria

A common problem for those who have to make sense of data which have been collected for the purpose of informing decision-making is what weight to give the different elements. Suppose 80 per cent of the users are satisfied with the timing of the dissemination of findings for those aspects of evaluation studies with which they are involved. Should this be seen as a positive achievement or a cause for concern? To some extent the conclusion drawn will depend on the context. If the satisfaction rating in the past has been around levels lower than 80 per cent, then this will represent an improvement. Similarly, if the satisfaction ratings for other issues being addressed by the self evaluation are less than 80 per cent, then satisfaction levels for timing would be seen in a relatively positive light. The only other sources of comparative data are external sources and data on such aspects as the quality of evaluation systems tend to be rare. The alternative approach is for specific target figures to have been agreed. Where this is the case, the initial targets are likely to be based on projections from current levels.

The problems are somewhat different with qualitative data. The data can give insight into problems with processes and explanations for unexpected outcomes. The problems arise between the tendency to generalize and to quantify on the one hand, and the tendency to give undue weight to evidence which accords with the interpreter's own tacit knowledge about the issue. John Brennan (1993) describes the process in relation to institutional self-assessment:

> Academic peer 'experts' may largely discount assembled information, preferring to use a mixture of reputational and tacit professional knowledge in reaching judgements. In such cases the assessment process becomes opaque to all but the expert insiders. At the other extreme, information can be converted into performance indicators by the mechanistic application of pre-determined formulae, leaving virtually no 'space' for judgement by anybody.

The issue about 'space' for judgement is an important one, not least because it presents many difficulties for those who have to make the judgements and defend their conclusions. Nevertheless, the sheer process of striving to agree standards and norms for key activities does provide those involved with the opportunity of making explicit their own perception of the standards for which the evaluation system should be aiming.

Extent of coverage

The greater the extent of devolution of evaluation activities which has occurred, the more of a problem is the decision about the extent of the coverage of any self-evaluation activity. Where the evaluation system is small and compact with a clearly defined membership, there are likely to be relatively few problems in bringing everyone's activities within the scope of the self-evaluation. However, where programme evaluation activities are to a large extent devolved and are carried out by a range of people on an occasional basis, the problem takes on a rather different dimension. Indeed, the extent of the devolution and the amount and type of evaluation work undertaken by different staff may well form one of the issues being reviewed.

Sources and means of collection

As with other evaluation activities, there are many different sources of data which can be drawn on for the self-evaluation exercise:

- records of requests for evaluation work;
- records of organizational commitments to evaluation activities;

- reports of dissemination exercises;
- evaluation reports;
- minutes of meetings discussing findings and utilization of findings;
- group discussions for evaluators;
- feedback forms from users;
- extended interviews with key users.

The data for the self-evaluation exercise then can come from any source which is verifiable. The means of collecting that data can be equally diverse, and will depend to a considerable extent on the frequency and duration of each of the exercises. If there is time enough and resources enough for data to be specially sought through small specially designed studies or surveys, then data can be sought from the most appropriate sources. If the self-evaluation is seen as a relatively marginal activity, then accessible existing data and easily collected and processed data (such as monitoring key users' views and evaluators' own perceptions) will have to form the basis of the data from which conclusions are drawn.

Frequency and duration of self-evaluations

There are a number of ways of approaching the design and organization of the self-evaluation. Each has different benefits and costs (see Figure 9.1).

Clearly the less frequently it is carried out, the more intrusive it is likely to be. The benefit of carrying out self-evaluation on an ongoing basis is that the collection and analysis of data for the purposes of self-evaluation will be seen as routine. The danger is that the issues of concern may vary as the context for the evaluation work varies and so the issues addressed by the on-going monitoring may not reflect current major areas of concern. In a similar sense, the data which is collected would have to be relatively easy to collect and analyse in order to maintain the costs of the self-evaluation at a sustainable level.

Frequency	Benefits	Costs
ongoing	routinized system	non-specific
occasional frequent	schedule ahead	vulnerable priority
occasional infrequent	commitment of special effort	intrusive

Figure 9.1 *Frequency and duration of self-evaluations*

Where self-evaluation is carried out on an occasional basis, it can be easier to set up special studies to investigate specific concerns. However, the danger must be that unless it has been allocated a high priority by the organization, it may well be vulnerable to delay if other problems requiring an input from the evaluation system emerge. Deferment is less likely to happen if the self-evaluation occurs only on an infrequent basis. Special resources are likely to have been allocated for the exercise if it is driven either within the organization but external to the evaluation system, or external to the organization. However a major one-off exercise is also far more likely to be intrusive in its effect on staff and on the work of the system in that the data needed and the information required from staff are less likely to be collated and held as a matter of routine.

What are the resource implications?

There can be a tension between the need to monitor and review the work of a system in order to maximize its effectiveness and its efficiency and the need to minimize the costs of achieving that efficiency. At the beginning of Chapter 1 it was pointed out that we all evaluate our own actions in a variety of ways, but that for the most part it is in an ad hoc and informal manner. Similarly within a learning system, individual members will be evaluating their own work and the work of others in order to improve their chances of achieving their own work objectives. For the organization to be seen as a learning organization, it needs to give a clear message to its employees that the activities which comprise self-evaluation are seen as essential to the health of the organization. The allocation of a specific resource for that area of activity is a way of showing a clear and explicit commitment to it.

Realistically, however, any allocation of resource to this activity is likely to be relatively marginal. We have talked of an investment in organizational terms of between 5 and 7 per cent for evaluation purposes. If the allocation for the self-evaluation of a system were to differ markedly from that sort of percentage, it would probably be with a specific purpose in mind. At such levels, the costs are relatively marginal; nevertheless, resources in the form of staff support and staff time, data collection and analysis assistance, and above all time for dissemination and reflection about how best to utilize the findings will need to be recognized and made available. The evaluation system should, like Caesar's wife, aim not only to use evaluation as it wishes other parts of the organization to use evaluation, but it must be seen publicly to be prepared to practise what it preaches.

References

AAU (1991) *Study on Cost Effectiveness and Efficiency in African Universities: A Synthesis Report*, Accra-North, Ghana: AAU (PO Box 5744).

Abbott-Chapman, J et al (1992) *Monitoring Student Progress*, Youth Education Studies Centre, University of Tasmania.

Ashby, A (1992) *Analysis of Student and Course Retention Rates by Educational Group (1988-92)*, mimeo: Student Research Centre, Open University, Milton Keynes.

Argyris, C and Schön, D (1978) *Organizational Learning: A Theory of Action Perspective*, Reading, Mass: Addison-Wesley.

Beattie, A (1987) *Pandora's Box? Multiple Agendas in Local Inter-agency Workshops in Community Care: An Ethnographic Evaluation, from the Researcher's Perspective*, King's Fund/ Local Boroughs Training Committee, mimeo.

Beattie, A (1993) *Figuring out the Quality of Open University Services: A Report on an Exploratory Study in 3 Regions*, SRC Report No 8, Milton Keynes: IET, Open University.

Brennan, J (1993) *Institutional Self-assessment: Overview Paper*, London: Quality Support Centre, Open University.

Brookfield, S (1986) *Understanding and Facilitating Adult Learning*, Milton Keynes: Open University Press.

Brown, S (1990) *It Ain't What You Do It's the Way that You Do It*, conference paper presented at Teleteaching 90, WCCE/90 Associated mini-conference, 9–13 July, Sydney.

Calder, J (1992) *Breadth or Depth: Reflections on Quality Measurement from the Open University*, paper presented to the 4th International Conference on Assessing Quality in Higher Education, Enschede: University of Twente.

Calder, J (1993) 'Adult learning and success', in: Calder J (ed), *Disaffection and Diversity: Overcoming Barriers for Adult Learners*, London: Falmer.

Cameron, S and Holloway, J (1992) *Review and Development of MBA Quality Issue Card System*, internal memo, Open Business School, Open University, Milton Keynes.

Cope, R and Hannah, W (1975) *Revolving College Doors*: John Wiley.

Copeland, P (1988) 'Interactive video: what the research says', *Media in Education and Development*, **21**, pp 60–3.

Daniel, J (1989) 'The worlds of open learning', in: Paine, N (ed), *Open Learning in Transition*, London: Kogan Page.

Drucker, P (1979 [1968]) *The Practice of Management*, London: Pan.

Farnes, N, Woodley, A, and Ashby, A (1993) *Evaluation of Open Business School Courses in Hungary: Report on a Workshop held at Eurocontact June 17–18 1993*, Milton Keynes: Student Research Centre Report, Open University.

Finol, J B (1992) 'A distance teaching training model for Venezuela petroleum and petrochemicals industries', in: *Conference Abstracts: Distance Education for the Twenty-First Century*. Thailand: International Council for Distance Education, Sukhothirat Open University.

Flagg, B (1990) *Formative Evaluation for Educational Technologies,* Hillsdale, NJ: Lawrence Erlbaum Associates.

Freeman, R (1991) 'Quality assurance in learning materials production', *Open Learning*, November.

Grant, J et al (1992) *Formal Opportunities in Postgraduate Education for Hospital Doctors in Training: Full Report of a Research Study commissioned by SCOPME*, London: Standing Committee On Postgraduate Medical Education.

Guttentag, M and Saar, S (1977) 'Introduction', in: Guttentag, M and Saar, S (eds), *Evaluation Studies Review Annual Vol 2*, Beverley Hills: Sage.

Halliday, S (1993) 'BS5750: never mind the quality', *The Observer*, 14 March.

Harris, D and Dochy, F (1990) 'Theoretical considerations and practical pitfalls: the use of performance indicators', in: Docky, F, Segers, M, and Wijnen, W (eds), *Management Information and Performance Indicators in Higher Education: An International Issue*, Assen/Maastricht: Van Gorcum.

Handy, C (1990) *The Age of Unreason*, London: Arrow.

Innes, S (1989) 'The Open College: a personal view', in: Paine, N (ed), *Open Learning in Transition*, London: Kogan Page.

Jeynes, J (1990) 'The effectiveness of a standard management training package in an industrial setting', in: Farmer, E, Eascott, D and Lantz, B (eds), *Aspects of Educational and Training Technology Vol XX111: Making Open Learning Systems Work*, London: Kogan Page.

Jones, A, Kirkup, G and Kirkwood, A (1992) *Personal Computers for Distance Education*, London: Paul Chapman.

Kirkwood, A (1992) 'Interaction upon interaction: combining interactive video and group sessions in management training', *Computers in Adult Education and Training*, **2**, 3 pp 174–85.

Kogan, M (1989) *Evaluating Higher Education*, London: Jessica Kingsley.

Moodie, G and Nation, D (1993) 'Reforming a system of distance education', in: Evans, T and Nation, D (eds), *Reforming Open and Distance Education: Critical Reflections from Practice*, London: Kogan Page.

Morris, A (1990) *Performance Indicators. Report of a Committee of Enquiry*, London: Polytechnics and Colleges Funding Council.

Mouli, C Raja and Ramakrishna, C Pushpa (1991) 'Readability of distance education course material', in *Research into Distance Education*, Athabasca, October.

Nathenson, M, and Henderson, E (1976) 'Developmental testing: a new beginning', *Teaching at a Distance*, **7**.

Newsam, P (1993) 'To err is only human, after all', *The Times Educational Supplement*, 25 June.

Nunan, T (1992) *Student Feedback for the Evaluation of Distance Teaching and Learning*, mimeo, Distance Education Centre, University of South Australia.

Pacey, L (1992) *Strategic Planning and Open Learning: Turkey Tails and Frogs*, paper presented at the World Conference on Distance Education, Bangkok: The International Council in Distance Education.

Paine, N (1990) Review of 'The Open Tech Programme Development Review – Final Report', *Open Learning*, June.

Parlett, M and Hamilton, D (1981) 'Evaluation as illumination: a new approach to the study of innovatory programs' (originally published as Occasional Paper Number Nine, University of Edinburgh Centre for Research in the Educational Sciences, 1972), in: Parlett, M and Dearden, G (eds), *Introduction to Illuminative Evaluation: Studies in Higher Education*, SRHE, University of Surrey, Guilford.

Paul, R (1990) 'Towards a new measure of success: developing independent learners', *Open Learning*, February.

Richmond, J M and Daniel, J (1979) *Evaluation of the Educational Experiments on the Hermes Satellite 1976-77: Final Report*, Edmonton, Alberta: Athabasca University.

Robinson, B (1992) *Applying Quality Standards in Open and Distance Education*, paper presented at the International Conference on Quality,

Standards and Research in European Distance Education, Sweden: European Association of Distance Teaching Universities.

Rowntree, D (1977) *Assessing Students: How Shall we Know Them?* London: Harper & Row.

Sahlin, E (1992) 'Mixed mode courses to meet the demands of transition', in: *Conference Abstracts: Distance Education for the Twenty-First Century*, Thailand: International Council for Distance Education, Sukhothirat Open University.

SATURN (1992) *SATURN Quality Guide: Pilot Edition*, Amsterdam: SATURN (Keizersgracht 756, 1017EZ Amsterdam, The Netherlands).

Schramm, W (1977) 'Foreword', in: Bates, T and Robinson, J (eds), *Evaluating Educational Television and Radio*, Milton Keynes: Open University Press.

Scriven, M (1976) 'The methodology of evaluation', in: *Perspectives in Curriculum Evaluation*, AERA Monograph No 1.

Stufflebeam, D et al (1971) *Educational Evaluation and Decision-making*, Itasca, Ill: Peacock.

Swift, B (1992) *MBA Audit 1992: Progress Report and Initial Survey Results*, Internal Report, Student Research Centre, Open University, Milton Keynes.

Swift, B and Swarbrick, A (1983) 'Needs of women technologists', internal report, Institute of Educational Technology, Open University.

Tavistock Institute of Human Relations (1987) *The Open Tech Development Review: Final Report*, London: The Tavistock Institute of Human Relations.

Tessmer, M (1993) *Planning and Conducting Formative Evaluations: Improving the Quality of Education and Training*, London: Kogan Page.

Thorpe, M (1993) *Evaluating Open and Distance Learning*, (2nd edn), Harlow: Longman Group.

Underwood, A (1991) *Total Quality Management (TQM) - The Theory*, Seminar on the theory and practice of Total Quality Management, BDMO, Open University, Milton Keynes, November.

Westerheijden, D, Weusthof, P and Fredericks, M (1992) *Effects of Self-Evaluations and Visiting Committees: A Survey of Quality Management in Dutch Higher Education*, paper presented to the 4th International Conference on Assessing Quality in Higher Education, Enschede: Centre for Higher Education Policy Studies, University of Twente.

Woodcock, A C (1990) 'Practical problems encountered in producing distance learning material for higher education', in: Farmer, E, Eascott, D and Lantz, B (eds), *Aspects of Educational and Training Technology Vol XX111: Making Open Learning Systems Work*, London: Kogan Page.

Woodley, A and Ashby, A (1993) 'Target audience: assembling a profile of your learners', in: Lockwood, F (ed), *Materials Production in Open and Distance Leaning*, London: Paul Chapman.

Woodley, A and Macintosh, N (1980) *The Door Stood Open: An Evaluation of the Open University Younger Student Pilot Scheme*, London: Falmer.

Zand, H (1993) 'Developmental testing: monitoring academic quality and teaching effectiveness', in: Lockwood, F (ed), *Materials Production in Open and Distance Leaning*, London: Paul Chapman.

Index